The Spirit of Adoption

The Spirit of Adoption

Writers on Religion, Adoption, Faith, and More

edited by
MELANIE SPRINGER MOCK,
MARTHA KALNIN DIEDE,
and JEREMIAH WEBSTER

foreword by
JOHN J. MESKE

CASCADE *Books* • Eugene, Oregon

THE SPIRIT OF ADOPTION
Writers on Religion, Adoption, Faith, and More

Copyright © 2014 Wipf and Stock Publishers. All rights reserved. Except for brief quotations in critical publications or reviews, no part of this book may be reproduced in any manner without prior written permission from the publisher. Write: Permissions, Wipf and Stock Publishers, 199 W. 8th Ave., Suite 3, Eugene, OR 97401.

Cascade Books
An Imprint of Wipf and Stock Publishers
199 W. 8th Ave., Suite 3
Eugene, OR 97401

www.wipfandstock.com

ISBN 13: 978-1-62564-076-5

Cataloguing-in-Publication data:

The spirit of adoption : writers on religion, adoption, faith, and more / edited by Melanie Springer Mock, Martha Kalnin Diede, and Jeremiah Webster ; foreword by John J. Meske.

xx + 148 pp. ; 23 cm. Includes bibliographical references.

ISBN 13: 978-1-62564-076-5

1. Adoption—Religious aspects—Christianity. I. Mock, Melanie Springer, 1968–. II. Diede, Martha Kalnin. IV. Webster, Jeremiah. V. Meske, John J. VI. Title.

BT165 .S68 2014

Manufactured in the U.S.A.

"Kiki," by Kohleun Adamson, was previously published in *Relief* 3.2 (2009) and is used by permission of its author.

"Dumb Questions about Adoption," by Klarissa I. Clark, was previously published in *Viewpoint* (Fall 2012) and is used by permission of its author.

All scripture quotations, unless otherwise indicated, are taken from the Holy Bible, New International Version®, NIV®. Copyright ©1973, 1978, 1984, 2011 by Biblica, Inc.™ Used by permission of Zondervan. All rights reserved worldwide. www.zondervan.com. The "NIV" and "New International Version" are trademarks registered in the United States Patent and Trademark Office by Biblica, Inc.

Contents

Contributors vii

Foreword by John J. Meske xiii

Preface xv

Introduction: The Spirit of Adoption
—Melanie Springer Mock xvii

1. Trinitarian Adoption and Identity Formation
   —*Geordie Ziegler* 1
2. Our Mutual Adoption—*Martha Kalnin Diede* 8
3. Found by Grace—*Forrest Inslee* 14
4. When Adoption, Colorado Ranches, and *Kung Fu Panda* Collide—*Jeremy Cook* 21
5. How Adoption Brought Me from Darkness to Light
   —*Maggie Lalich* 29
6. The Right Fit?—*Elizabeth Huston* 34
7. Kiki—*Kohleun Adamson* 37
8. On (Not) Fearing the Mystery of God
   —*Melanie Springer Mock* 42
9. Overcoming—*Jere Witherspoon* 50
10. Where in the Bible Am I?—*Kimberly Claassen Felton* 64
11. The *Whole* Story: Revisiting the Unspoken Complexities of Adoption—*Jacqueline N. Gustafson* 70
12. The Fruitful Tree—*David Michael Haslet* 87
13. Adoption of Lizette—*Moses Harris* 97

Contents

14	Love or Luck?—*Douglas Webster*	102
15	All Shall Be Well—*Jeremiah Webster*	107
16	Open Questions—*Michael Dean Clark*	114
17	Dumb Questions about Adoption —*Klarissa I. Clark* (Age 10)	118
18	Grit and Grace—*Beth Woolsey*	121
19	A Tapestry of Redemption: One Adoptee's Journey —*Kelli Hall*	125
20	Reflections on Adoption and Religion—*Russ Richter*	135
	Bibliography	147

Contributors

Kohleun Adamson grew up in Washington and Arizona before heading to Oregon to attend George Fox University where she studied philosophy and designed costumes for theater. After graduate school in the UK, Kohleun taught English at the college level. She currently lives in Oregon, working as a florist and freelance costume designer and editor, while developing cookie recipes and writing in her "spare time." She has tried to cut back on coffee.

Klarissa I. Clark is a young author of fiction and nonfiction mostly focused on mystery and climatic betrayal. At the age of nine, she published for the first time in *Viewpoint* magazine. She lives in San Diego with her parents and little brothers and is currently going into Dana Middle School. Klarissa wants to be a biologist after earning honors at Point Loma Nazarene University and write for fun when she grows up.

Michael Dean Clark is an author of fiction and nonfiction focused on loss and grace and redemption that doesn't look like we think it should. His work has appeared in *Fast Forward*, *Relief*, *Coach's Midnight Diner*, and elsewhere. Formerly an award winning journalist and high school English teacher, Clark now lives and writes in San Diego, California, with his wife and three children and works as a professor of writing at Point Loma Nazarene University.

Jeremy Cook is currently a Foundation and Corporate Development Specialist at Landesa, a Seattle nonprofit that works with governments to secure land rights for the world's poorest people. Previously he served for nine years with InterVarsity Christian Fellowship, first at Georgetown University and then in Kenya and France. His deep desire is to pastor a local church sometime in the next few years, so the next step is seminary, hopefully in Kenya, where he and his wife expect to help their adopted children further explore their story as transracially adopted children. Jeremy holds

Contributors

a BA in Political Science from The George Washington University and an MA in International Care & Community Development from Northwest University. He is an avid reader, podcast junkie, and slightly obsessed fan of the Washington Nationals.

Martha Kalnin Diede is a Senior Faculty Developer at the Coulter Faculty Commons at Western Carolina University. She published her first book, *Shakespeare's Knowledgeable Body*, upon invitation from Peter Lang, and her essays have appeared in journals and collections including *Christianity and Literary Theory* and *The WILLA Journal* among others. Her most recent essay appeared early in 2013 as part of a collection titled *Overcoming Adversity in Academe*. She has also produced three plays. She lives in Waynesville, North Carolina, with her husband and daughter, adopted from China at thirteen months. She is eagerly awaiting news on a pending adoption from Japan.

Kimberly Claassen Felton lives in Oregon with her husband and daughter. At the time of writing this essay, they were eager for the next Felton baby—waiting for a birth mom to choose them. Rather than fearing open adoption as she did the first time around, Kimberly now anticipates befriending the birth mom who chooses to entrust her with another child. Kimberly is a freelance writer and blogs regularly at NewlywedNoLonger.com.

Jacqueline N. Gustafson is Associate Professor and Dean of the School of Behavioral Sciences at California Baptist University. In addition, she leads study abroad courses throughout Europe. Her areas of scholarship include globalization and higher education, internationalization of curriculum, and study abroad. She is an avid global explorer and, along with her husband, she also enjoys exploring and creating world cuisines for family and friends.

Kelli Hall has a master's degree in social work and is a licensed social worker. She is passionate about her vocation as a mental health therapist specializing in adoption, foster care, and trauma related issues. Kelli lives in the Pacific Northwest with her husband and two children.

Moses Harris has been married for forty-one years to Ruby Jeanne Harris. He is an Ordained Elder with the Church of God in Christ and State Evangelist President for the Washington State Jurisdiction of the Church of

Contributors

God in Christ, and he runs his own 503(c) evangelistic association online where he provides weekly lessons and word studies in multiple languages at http://www.mosesharrisevangelisticassociation.org. In 1961, he graduated from Lincoln High School in Ruston, Louisiana. In 1976, he earned his PhD from the University of Washington in Romance Languages. In addition to his church leadership and his evangelistic association, he is also Professor of Modern Languages at Northwest University and has written several books. Importantly, he is also father to Lizette.

David Michael Haslet enjoys traveling, gardening, and martial arts. He can be found sword fighting with his son, singing "Baby Beluga" with his daughter, and hiking with his wife of eight years. Haslet currently teaches public high school art and engineering design, keeping a working suburban homestead with fruit trees, vegetable garden, and two egg-laying hens. He lives with his wife and two children in the Bay Area of California.

Elizabeth Huston is an early career professional. She currently resides in the Seattle area and is surrounded by great friends with whom she has found a great fit. She calls them her family by choice.

Forrest Inslee is first and foremost a dad to his daughter, Kayra Grace. He is also a professor and chair of the Master of Arts in International Care and Community Development at Northwest University, where he is privileged to invest in the lives of young graduate students with a passion for social justice. Forrest holds an MA and PhD in Communication from Northwestern University, and an MA in Theological Studies from Regent College.

Maggie Lalich lives in the Clear Lake area of Houston, Texas. She is a mother of two, married to Andy Lalich, and currently teaches pre-K in Pearland, Texas. Mrs. Lalich loves gardening, traveling, and singing.

Melanie Springer Mock is a Professor of English at George Fox University, Newberg, Oregon. Her essays and reviews have appeared in *Christian Feminism Today, Adoptive Families, The Chronicle of Higher Education*, and *Mennonite World Review*, among other places. Her most recent book is *Just Moms: Conveying Justice in an Unjust World* (2011). She blogs about (and deconstructs) images of women embedded in evangelical popular culture at *Ain't I a Woman?* and at *FemFaith*. She lives in Dundee, Oregon, with her husband and two ten-year-old sons: Benjamin Quan, adopted from

Vietnam at seven months, and Samuel Saraubh, adopted from India at three years.

Russ Richter was born in rural San Antonio, Texas in 1964, the third of four sons. In 1976, he and his family moved to Houston. He graduated from Sam Houston State University with a Bachelor of Science degree in Computer Science and moved back to Houston where he began his career in the IT industry with a large computer corporation. He met Julie in 1998, and they married in 2001. They adopted their first daughter from China in 2005 and their second in 2010. They are members of Cinco Ranch Church of Christ in Katy, Texas.

Douglas Webster mentors future pastors at Beeson Divinity School in Birmingham, Alabama. He and his wife Virginia have served churches in Toronto, Bloomington, Denver, San Diego, and Manhattan. Their three children are married, and they have two grandchildren. Doug has authored several books including *Soulcraft: How God Shapes Us through Relationships*, and *Living in Tension: A Theology of Ministry*.

Jeremiah Webster lives in Kirkland, Washington, with his wife and two children. His writing has appeared in *North American Review*, *Beloit Poetry Journal*, *Crab Creek Review*, *Ruminate*, *The Midwest Quarterly*, *REAL*, *Dappled Things*, *Euonia Review*, *Rock and Sling*, and *Floating Bridge Review*. He also provided a critical introduction for *Paradise in The Waste Land* (Wiseblood Books), an anthology of poems by T. S. Eliot. When he isn't exploring the woods, fishing for rainbow trout, or listening to piano concertos, he is an Assistant Professor of English at Northwest University.

Jere Witherspoon was born in Wyoming in 1958. She was raised outside of San Ysidro, California, with her three siblings until the age of ten when her family moved to Cottage Grove, Oregon. There she became involved in 4-H, sports activities, and an active social life. She married Wade Witherspoon in 1978; they have three children and one grandchild together. Jere has worked at George Fox University for the past sixteen years.

Beth Woolsey is the writer and humorist behind the *Five Kids is a Lot of Kids* blog. She's been described by readers as "optimistic, authentic, poignant and laugh-out-loud funny, capturing the mom experience with all its pathos and humor." Beth and her husband, Greg, are parents to five kids. Their kids are adopted and homemade, singletons and multiples, and some have special needs. Most importantly, Beth says, "they're all our very own."

Geordie Ziegler and his wife, Sharon, have three children—Andrew (15), Brennan (13), and KaiLi (9)—and lived in Scotland from 2007 to 2013 while Geordie pursued a PhD in a Trinitarian theology of grace. As of August 2013, Geordie took up the position of pastor for adult discipleship and formation at Columbia Presbyterian Church in Vancouver, Washington. Geordie is an ordained minister in the PCUSA and Sharon has a master's from Regent College in Vancouver, BC, in marriage and family ministry.

Foreword

Love does not depend upon blood relation. Families who have united with their children through adoptive love have realized this very fact. Parents often comment on the threads connecting them and their children—whether biological or adopted. Adoptive parents frequently note birthdays that are the same as one of the parents or a family member. Perhaps they find the translation of the child's name connects to a parent or a family member. For people of faith, their adoption is a part of their fate and destiny, as it is a fulfillment of what God had planned for them and their children. Adoption is what was meant to be.

Families who choose to increase their families through adoption need to understand that the journey does not end once they receive their children. The journey is a lifelong one and will present each family with feelings of love, joy, happiness, sadness, and fear. These feelings are not limited to one family but are shared by all families.

When a family considers adoption, they must understand that the feelings of grief, loss, joy, happiness, sadness, and fear are part of their story. The birth mother who chooses life and adoption instead of abortion, abandonment, or institutionalization of her child may suffer from grief and loss in separating herself from her child but also may experience feelings of joy and happiness in knowing that her child has a loving family. The child who suffers from grief and loss in separating from the birth mother, guardian, or orphanage may feel fear in joining a new family but also experiences joy and happiness upon receiving the unconditional love given by the new family. The adoptive parents may suffer from grief and loss in not having a biological child, and may fear rejection by the child, but will also experience the joy and happiness that comes from loving their child.

Furthermore, the family must understand that not every step of the adoption process is entirely wonderful. The time necessary to unite with their child can be lengthened by many factors, such as a birth mother revoking her consent to allow the child to be adopted, or a country of origin suspending adoptions, or a country suspending adoptions of children in certain foreign countries.

One of the greatest gifts that God gives us is the gift of being a parent. Children unite with their parents in many ways, one of which is adoption. Through this gift each parent, child, and family member will experience great joy, happiness, sadness, and, most of all, love. Through all of the emotional ups and downs, family members will come to realize that they were meant to be together as a family and to experience these emotions together.

The stories presented here express the feelings of grief, loss, sadness, fear, joy, happiness, and love that people touched by adoption share. Birth parents, prospective adoptive parents, adoptees, and other family members will benefit from the stories presented here by hearing about the varying emotions experienced during the lifelong journey of adoption.

John J. Meske, Executive Director
Faith International Adoptions

Preface

"The unexamined life is not worth living."

—SOCRATES

By its very nature, experience is multifaceted. Like a refraction, each life travels along a unique path. No two are exactly alike, and a life informed by adoption is no different. The essays included in this volume represent a broad spectrum of experiences, backgrounds, and theological perspectives. As editors, our goal was to *set the table* and provide each author the freedom to share an adoption narrative without ideological restraint. When we did so, the project became less about advancing a single agenda and more about the sanctity that surrounds each individual made in the image of God.

We want to thank the contributors for their courage and winsome exploration of the *spirit of adoption*. Our prayer is that this collection will promote dialogue in service of the very real challenges that adoption presents to families and communities. This anthology resists the saccharine, the stereotype, and seeks habitation beyond the feckless rhetoric that often accompanies the adoption debate. These essays grapple with the question that was posed to Jesus in the Gospel of Luke: "Who is my neighbor?"

When adoption becomes the answer to this question, the outcome is one of humility and holiness, gravity and grace.

The Editors
2014

Introduction

The Spirit of Adoption

Melanie Springer Mock

I knew what was coming before the older woman said one word. I knew, and flinched—though she probably didn't notice, her eyes being focused so intently on my two boys, drinking their cozy hot chocolates at our local bookstore.

"Ohhhh," she sighed. "Your boys are adopted, aren't they?! Such beautiful children!" Benjamin and Samuel looked at her, vaguely smiling, made only a little uncomfortable by the old person looming over them.

And then she said it.

"What a great gift you have given them! What a great ministry! Saving them from what would have been a very bad life." She finally looked at me. "You must be a very dear person, to save them like that."

Even though a hundred strangers and more have made similar comments about my boys—and have presumed my family's story open to inquiry, because we look different from each other—I am still flummoxed when someone praises me for saving my children. I don't know the best way to respond. Sometimes, I offer a clichéd rejoinder, something like, "The gift is all mine!" Most often, I long to set nosy strangers aright, letting them know that my children are not a mission project, that *they* saved *me*, and that I am no better or worse than any other mother trying to do what's right by her children. I long to set them straight, that is, except I don't: my mama taught me to be polite, even to strangers, so I most often smile, then walk away.

What I want to tell nosy strangers like my bookstore inquisitor is this: my sons' adoption, any adoption, is a messy business, fraught with paradox

Introduction

and complication, with joy and sorrow, with loss and redemption. But the narrative of adoption in the United States, and particularly among evangelical Christians, has no room for this complexity. Adoptions are framed as happy affairs in which parents desiring children are matched with children needing homes; the children grow and flourish because "love is all they need"; and the birth mothers, honored for their worthy sacrifice, voluntarily slip into anonymity, allowing their offspring space to live happily ever after in their forever families.

In many evangelical churches, there is an overlay of biblical mandate to this happily-ever-after mythology, giving rise to a number of adoption ministries throughout the country. The scriptural imperative to help widows and orphans is strong, of course, but these well-meaning ministries also urge Christians to adopt as a way to—in the words of one organization—"build God's kingdom one child at a time." Thus adoption not only saves children from a lifetime without a family but also guarantees eternal life. Children adopted into Christian homes are assured their salvation—or, at least, are more assured of salvation than they would have been had they remained in their dark countries dominated by presumably heathen religions. Or so we are told.

It seems almost too cynical to question the cultural mythology of adoption, and almost too heretical to doubt the significance of adoption ministries that have placed thousands of children into loving homes. Aren't children better off with families than in orphanages? Shouldn't we laud birth mothers who, given the choice of adoption or abortion, choose the life-giving option? Isn't it wonderful that parents who cannot birth children can still become mothers and fathers? And doesn't the nature of adoption reflect God's love for all children?

Of course. And, maybe. And, potentially, no.

Because if you ask almost anyone who has experience with adoption, the answers are more complex, more paradoxical than our contemporary mythologies about adoption allow. Ask any adoptive parent who has struggled with attaching to her child and you discover that love isn't always enough to heal a child's brokenness. Ask a birth mother why she relinquished her baby and the answer will undoubtedly be freighted with her sense of loss and emptiness. Ask almost any grown adoptee what adoption has meant for him and he will likely admit to a complicated connection to his past, his birth culture and family, and his identity. And he will probably

Introduction

not want to be seen as a ministry or mission project, forever indebted to parents who "saved" him from his past.

The Spirit of Adoption explores many of the complexities inherent in adoption and its relationship to spirituality, challenging us to move beyond the common tropes about adoption to consider the more difficult questions adoption raises about the nature of God, of family, of culture, of loss and joy. This collection bears witness to the ways adoption shapes its participants' spiritual lives by asking those participants to share their own stories, in their own voices. By allowing others to narrate their spiritual journeys through adoption, we hope to proclaim adoption can be a wonderful, powerful, hopeful experience *and* one that is difficult, painful, despairing. And that these paradoxes of adoption might be held together in God's hand.

The essays in this anthology include those written by adoptive parents, most of whom made the intentional choice to invite children into their lives and their families, and whose lives are in many cases far different from birth parents, who relinquish their children, either by choice or by force. Because the stories of birth parents are too often absent from adoption narratives, we have made every effort to include their experiences here; their spiritual journeys, of creation and loss and sacrifice, are crucial to a more complete understanding of adoption—and, potentially, of God's nature. Perhaps most significantly, we have included the narratives of those most affected by adoption and its many complexities: the adopted themselves.

We recognize, of course, that these are only a microcosm of the many lives affected by adoption. Nearly 2 percent of all children in the United States today are adopted, which means innumerable more birth and adoptive parents, siblings, grandparents, and other relatives are also part of our communities. Each and every person's experience with adoption—and every person's spiritual journey—will reflect God's unique imprint. Thus, we hope *The Spirit of Adoption* will be a starting point for richer conversation about adoption and spirituality, and about the ways contemporary mythologies about adoption have failed to describe appropriately what adoption really is—or, if we are honest, who God is as well.

While I write this introduction, my ten-year-old sons are outside, playing with neighbors in the cul-de-sac. They are on the cusp of adolescence, still eager to cuddle with their parents and sleep with their pillow pets, though also intrigued by pop music, the girls in their classrooms, and, increasingly, their birth cultures and birth families. Both boys ask questions we can't begin to answer about those cultures and families, about their lives

Introduction

before we met them, but also about the presence of evil, the veracity of the Bible, and the nature of a God who, according to my eldest, "doesn't really do anything. Just sits there." (Because, you see, God failed to deliver on the million bucks my son was hoping for.)

As they straddle this space between childhood and adulthood, between innocence and experience, I want them to know there are others who have been on journeys similar to their own and who have asked similar questions about adoption and about God. I also want them to know that being their mother fills me with joy, although I recognize that my joy comes with loss: to their birth families, who have lost the opportunity to raise amazing boys; and to themselves, as they have lost the chance to grow in their native cultures, surrounded by people who look like them.

More than anything else, though, I want them—and all who read *The Spirit of Adoption*—to know that God stands in the midst of that joy and of that loss. For I believe those who receive this message will develop a richer understanding of adoption, and of God as well.

1

Trinitarian Adoption and Identity Formation

GEORDIE ZIEGLER

Blind Faith

We had committed our entire lives to her before we'd ever met her; and we'd committed her future to us. She, who had absolutely no claim or connection to us, no biological, geographical, or relational connection, had passively received more commitment from me than close friends I had known for decades. This was indeed a leap of faith. Yes, we had a picture—a very unattractive one at that—of an overstuffed, tightly bundled, Buddha-like straight-faced infant mercilessly placed in a basket of fake fruit for what was intended to be a photographer's artistic masterpiece.

October 11, 2004: "Gotcha Day." The initial meeting and handover was far from joyous. Frankly, her vacant stare shocked and scared us. She seemed impervious to her surroundings, completely absent of all emotional affect. I'd never seen this sort of behavior before, and her blank face rekindled all my worries about severe attachment disorders and inability to bond. What, I wondered, had we gotten ourselves into? Were we really ready for this? What if this vacant gaze which is her countenance is all there is? Can I love a child who can't even see me—who when she looks at me looks right through me? These thoughts flashed through my mind in the first moments of our meeting, yet there was little time to ponder and still less to share them with my family members. We had papers to sign, footprints to stamp, and doctors' assessments to complete.

This moment was not our first jolt in the process. Only six weeks into our "paper pregnancy," which began on November 11, 2003, the move toward adoption had already caused an extended family split. Questions about financial "wisdom" (or lack thereof) and parental (in)competence mushroomed into an all-out war with one of my siblings. While the adoption event was simply an opportunity for long-standing family of origin issues to emerge, I could not help sensing the irony of dealing with the rejection of a blood sibling over the decision to include an outsider through adoption.

All this and much more swirled in my mind as those first few days of getting acquainted with my new daughter unfolded. Could I love this child who is "not mine" in the same way that I loved my two "natural" sons? How would my feelings for her compare to my feelings for them? How long would it take for me to love this child with my heart as well as with my signature on government papers?

The answer came in less than forty-eight hours. Somehow the love I feared I might not have in me appeared. I say "appeared" because the only way I can explain it is as a mystery whose origin is somehow outside of myself. My family and I took her to a restaurant for dinner that first night and discovered the food she likes and how she likes to be fed. We took her to the local zoo and watched the bears-riding-motorcycles show, and I saw her first laugh. I loved her before I knew her, yet I also fell in love with her and the person she slowly revealed herself to be. And my father's heart grew in a way I'd never known before—a fierce commitment to guard and care for this child of *mine*, no matter what might come.

Adoption by Grace, and so by Law

This experience of adopting and the new feelings that I found emerging within my soul led me to begin reflecting anew on the way that New Testament writers use the concept of adoption. Somehow, though I'd been a Christian for nearly thirty years, I'd missed the magic in the metaphor. Granted, this is not hard to do, particularly in a church culture that prides itself on the "logic" of legal or forensic images to describe the human's relation to God. Certainly, any adoption has some legal elements: fees to pay, forms to fill out, assessments to undergo, and governments to satisfy. Yet the requirements of legal language do not sum up the meaning of adoption. This is because, fundamentally, the legal necessities do not make the adoption happen. They may make it official, but in reality they only confirm that to which the heart has already given itself.

This is true in marriage as well. Society has two forms of marriage (represented by a judge and a minister), and while they usually go together, they carry vastly different meanings. For human beings who live in a fallen world, society requires an accountability to our commitments that prevents us from switching our allegiances too easily. Thus, modern marriage involves a judge and lawyers. I once performed a wedding for a couple who never registered their marriage with the state. They wanted to get married, but the state paperwork was set up to punish them for getting married. So I agreed to marry them in the church, before God, and without any state involvement. Pastorally, this took some discernment: I needed to be sure that they recognized that the covenant they were making to one another before God was binding. It was not the state or a string of legal obligations that would hold them together should their feelings change, but Christ.

Now I should add that I am truly thankful for the legal paperwork. I'm thankful that there is a system that protects me from anyone coming along and arguing that KaiLi is not my daughter. I'm thankful that a paper trail proves that she is indeed mine. These days my family and I do a lot of international traveling, and without this paperwork she could not come with us. Without any genetic link, government paperwork is all we have to prove that she is ours. We ran into this recently when applying for a new UK visa. Because KaiLi was not our daughter by biology, we needed to provide the United Kingdom Border Agency paper evidence to prove that KaiLi was indeed legally adopted and belonged to us. So the paperwork has a purpose and a place, but it is far from the thing itself. What bonds me to KaiLi is love and commitment, that is, a *decision*.

These thoughts have caused me to reconsider my understanding of the nature of God, in particular what exactly bonds me to God. Because the fact is that although there may be times (like crossing national borders) when others may require me to show the paperwork that proves she is mine, the paperwork is not what makes KaiLi my daughter. If this is so on the human level, how does this work on the divine? Obviously, I can't discover what God is like by manufacturing a larger version of myself, but I can't escape the fact that my own experience with adoption challenges some of my long-held assumptions about the nature of my relationship with God.

Teaching Orphans to Say "Abba!"

Significantly, every time the New Testament speaks of adoption, it speaks of adoption to *sonship*, a term that carries the strong connotation of rights and privileges of a child within the family. Even when the specific word for adoption (*huioqesia*) is not actually used, the metaphor is still present in the background. All references to our being "sons" and "children" of God speak of the same reality. Because in the first century only men could hold property, to be adopted was to be "placed as a son" within a family system. In first-century culture, adoption preserved the estate of the deceased. While the slave could not inherit the owner's property, the son would. "Sonship" is not sexist language; it is about receiving a relationship that comes entirely as gift.

In the New Testament, sonship is the product of a double sending. First, God sends his Son to live as one of us, and second, God sends the Spirit of his Son into our hearts, crying, "Abba!" (Gal 4:6; Rom 8:15). What we so often miss is the fact that it is the Spirit of God who cries out to God. Yes, it is our hearts and our vocal chords that act, but they only do so derivatively. The cry "Abba, dear Father" is a God-generated cry. It is a cry from our own lips that manifests that we are members of God's family by adoption. In other words, adoption is most fundamentally a metaphor for *sharing*.

Only Jesus Christ himself is God's dear Son, and only he has the right to call God "Father." Yet because we are adopted sons and daughters, what is true of the Son of God is also extended to us. Baptized into Christ, you and I receive the Spirit of Christ, the Spirit of adoption who enables us to take up his cry of "Abba!" to the Father and share in his sonship. And the guarantee of our adoption is not legal paperwork, but the Spirit sent from the Son who unites us to himself. He is the true Son, the firstborn, but as his adopted brothers and sisters by grace, we share in his inheritance as "fellow-heirs" with Christ.

Now, if adoption is about sharing or participating in Jesus' relationship with his Father, then it is clearly about more than receiving the benefits of Christ. For example, adoption for our daughter KaiLi does not simply mean she receives the benefits of status as a U.S. citizen, or more material comforts. Nor is adoption primarily a legal declaration that transfers her from the Middle Kingdom of China to the new kingdom of the United States. She doesn't join our family because we pitied her or to get stuff. She joins the family—in order to be part of *the family*.

Adoption is not an instrument in a process toward an end goal beyond the family. The point of adoption is full participation in familial relations. If she were to think of her status in the family as a means to get stuff from us, rather than as a beloved child who shares in and is heir to all that we are and have, then her entire experience in the family would be warped and reduced to instrumentalism. More concisely put, she is who she is *in* the family, rather than *through* the family. Of course, material benefits come with adoption, but the real benefit of adoption is the family *itself*, not something else out there.

Adoption and the Way of Grace

What if we understood being a child of God in the same way? What if being a child of God is not simply being checked into the orphanage of the church, but being adopted into the family of the Trinity? Adoption does not simply create a new set of one-on-one relationships; it constitutes a dynamic fellowship in the communion of life and love (and squabbling) that is the family. When I think of the new thing that is our family this side of adoption, I am led to wonder about what it actually means to be in relationship with God through Christ in the fellowship of the Spirit. Clark Pinnock writes, "God has not left us outside the circle of his life. We are invited inside the Trinity as joint heirs together with Christ. By the Spirit we cry 'Abba' together with the Son, as we are drawn into the divine filial relationship and begin to participate in God's life."[1] The idea of adoption as Trinitarian adoption or as participation in the triune communion seems radically different than the metaphor evoked by the old "I have decided to follow Jesus" chorus I learned growing up. A God who adopts human beings means that God has somehow chosen not to be God without humanity, that in some amazing grace-like way, we are now included in the life of the man Jesus in his life with God.

How might this way of reimagining our relation to God remake our daily lives? How might it reshape how we think, how we relate, how we love ourselves, others, God, and the world? With an eye on the practical implications of adoption as our identity, Julie Canlis writes,

1. Pinnock, *Flame of Love*, 153.

The Spirit of Adoption

> The category of adoption reminds the church that its primary profession is to be sons and daughters, and that ethics—no different from the church's triune identity—also flows from this participation in God. Obedience takes on the cast of expressing our filial love for the Father, sanctification becomes living more deeply into this identity as children, prayer is a right because he is Father, and freedom rather than fear marks those who are "sons."[2]

To be adopted is to have a new identity, an identity that we did not make ourselves. No one adopts himself or herself. We are adopt*ed*. Yet what begins as a movement from outside of ourselves eventually remakes us as we learn to participate in our new identity as adopted children. This means that we cannot look to ourselves to know the truth about ourselves. As an adopted child, KaiLi does not look to herself to define the truth about herself; rather, she begins with the truth of herself-in-the-Ziegler-family. What she was not by nature, she is by grace, and through grace this identity becomes natural. This may take some time at first for the child brought into a new family, but just as one cannot be a little pregnant or a little married, neither can one be a little adopted. Now that she is in the family, she truly is one of us, fully included whether she feels like it or not. She is not a slave or a stepchild, but a child with all the rights and responsibilities and love of our two boys who are ours by biology as well as by grace.

The fact that we exist in an adopted relationship to God means that natural origin (i.e., biological parenthood) is not the most significant aspect of human existence. In fact, the opposite is true. Being born and thus existing merely provides the external basis for a history that is essentially a participation in various covenant relationships. We become what we are through active participation in the respective relations. Procreation without adoption/election is merely external. This is not how God parents God's children. St. Paul tells us that God the Father chose us in Christ before the creation of the world and that "in love he predestined us for adoption to sonship through Jesus Christ, in accordance with his pleasure and will" (Eph 1:3–5). In other words, God adopts us simply because God loves us, that is, God loves us *before* adopting us. And so God adopts us because doing so is a great joy and pleasure. And the reason God does this is that he loves to share his love. This sharing of God's love with us is what we call grace.

Thus, while adoption is an act of God for us in grace, that adoption, that determination, that election of God in Christ needs to be confirmed,

---

2. Canlis, *Calvin's Ladder*, 149–50.

accepted, elected, and adopted by our living by faith in that election and union with Christ. We need to embrace our adoption. So it is with the child. The child must also choose her parents by adopting them, in the same way that the parents have chosen. This unity is not created by blood but by the Spirit of God. It is an electing that keeps on electing and so increases the bond. My daughter embraces her adoption. We play a game called "I love you more," in which we keep upping the ante of love—"I love you all the way to the moon and back"; "well," I will say, "I love you to the stars." This game is fun because I always win with the trump card: I loved her first. And so does God: "We love because he first loved us" (1 John 4:19).

One of the comments I get quite regularly from strangers when they hear that KaiLi was adopted (obviously) from China is some variation on "She is so lucky." For me personally, I put this in the annoying comments category, right next to "How kind of you to save that child from a life of poverty and misery and atheism in a communist land." The honest truth is, *we* are the lucky ones. We didn't adopt our daughter in order to save her. We adopted her because *a*) we knew there was a need, and *b*) God gave us the desire to adopt. I love the way Frederick Buechner speaks of vocation: "The place God calls you to is the place where your deep gladness and the world's deep hunger meet."[3] That's all it was. We knew there was a need, and over time as we meditated on that need God converted "somebody should do something about this" to "we would love to do this." In the end, there was nothing noble in our choice to adopt. It was grace through and through—grace upon us giving us a sense of desire, and grace upon KaiLi meeting her need for a family. This again is how God works—by the grace of a heart full of love, not by the law of obligations and "you shoulds."

My wife and I have three children, two of whom are our biological offspring. Yet the fact is that being a parent to my kids is not really about me being the biological source of their genetic codes; more important, it is the fact that I chose and elected them and *keep on* choosing and electing them. In this way, all true parenting is an adoption, a grace—a choosing of *this one* as my own—in action, in relationship, in self-giving. Yet, I have found that in adoption there is an extra joy, an added parental pleasure. There is the fact that we chose this. We have the awareness of having used our God-given freedom well. And with that awareness we experience a corresponding desire to remain open to the faith walk, knowing that to walk with Jesus truly is fullness of joy because we have tasted it *here*.

3. Buechner, *Wishful Thinking*, 119.

2

Our Mutual Adoption

MARTHA KALNIN DIEDE

Adoption begins with loss. Transitioning into a "forever family," adopted children first lose their birth families and then any familiar caregivers; some lose a language as well. Many adoptive parents worry about their adopted children—how to parent the child through recognition, understanding, and acceptance of that loss. That our adopted daughter can fully recognize, understand, and accept her great losses has never been a particular worry of mine or of my spouse, for we understand loss and will do our best to help her understand it, too. Our own path to adoption also began with loss, and with a very pregnant neighbor in a teeny-weeny bikini. Aware of loss on both sides, but also of gain, we began our part of our daughter's adoption.

After trying for a year to become pregnant on our own, we sought infertility help and even achieved pregnancy—one that lasted six weeks. All the while, our next-door neighbor—wearing a bikini that emphasized her growing baby bump—blissfully sunned herself in the back yard. Seeing her pregnant and seeing her baby swelled our hopes for children. My frustration with our paper pregnancy mounted as she became pregnant again, and delivered, and became pregnant again, and delivered. All the while we lived with loss and waiting. To deal with the loss of our biological baby, we each drew on the coping mechanisms that we had developed over years, for by the time I became pregnant, I had buried my father, my favorite great-aunt, two of my grandparents, and several other relatives whom I held in varying degrees of closeness. Charles, my spouse, had buried his father and mother, multiple aunts and uncles, and all of his grandparents. Loss is like waiting: the way out is through, not around. So when we lost our baby, we found ourselves in different rooms each crying separately. And then we met in the kitchen.

Charles asked me, "Were you crying just now?"

I looked at him and asked, "Were you?"

And then we both laughed. Instead of grieving separately, we could grieve together—a choice that is psychologically much smarter.

But then came the real questions: What were we to do now? What had our real goal been in pursuing pregnancy? How important was the biological connection? Were our genes so phenomenal that we just *had* to keep them going? Or was our goal simply to parent a child regardless of genetic connection? Before we married, we had idealistically discussed adoption. Now we had a "real" discussion.

Charles said, "Girl."

I replied, "China."

At that moment, we decided to love a little Chinese girl, although as it turns out, she wasn't born yet. So we began the process of adopting.

The privacy and financial losses inherent in the process of international adoption beggar the imagination. Charles and I joked that the Chinese government soon knew more about us than the Internal Revenue Service. Stacks of paperwork to document everything about us from medical status to yearly salary moved from office to office. Our privacy went into the mail with checks that emptied our savings account. At the other end of those papers and payments was, we hoped and prayed, a little girl to make us parents.

Soon uncomfortable reality settled in. No matter how often we filed renewal paperwork, no matter how many trips we made to the Department of Homeland Security for fingerprinting, we could not make the process move any faster. We simply waited and hoped for our little girl. With the waiting wearing on us and on our agency, the agency became certified to place special needs children. We asked to switch piles. So we began a new set of paperwork for a child with minor correctable special needs. Still we waited. Three and a half years of waiting. Charles earned his MBA. I wrote a book.

Then one day our phone rang at 6:30 AM. Our adoption agency told us that they had a match: a little girl with a heart murmur. We had forty-eight hours to decide. So I printed out the file and took it with me to the final choir rehearsal before a Christmas concert. I sat in the parking lot under one of the lights, the file laid before me, listening intently to a doctor from the University of Washington Center for Adoption Medicine read it through, explaining the Chinese notations and the tiny EKG printout. I was late to rehearsal. I took the file with me to rehearsal so that the pediatrician who sang next to me could offer her expert opinion. Between pieces, she read the paperwork. Then, she smiled. "That looks like a fine babe. All of this other, well, this is just uninteresting." And I knew that we would say yes, pay the remaining thousands of dollars, and fly to China. We sent a care package to the little girl with a mosquito bite in the middle of her forehead who smiled at the camera. However, we did not realize that our little girl lived with a foster family and would not receive our package until six days before we arrived. So, although we followed the advice of the adoption books and sent her a package of pictures of us and our cats, and a blanket that smelled like us and our house, our package didn't reach our little girl in good time. And she hated the panda bear in the package.

With plane tickets, duplicate packets, and visas, we flew to Kunming, a provincial capital of six million people. After our last childless night, which we had spent mostly imagining ourselves as parents, we put ourselves at the mercy of our guide and driver, who took us to the Children's Welfare Center. Although the temperature was about seventy degrees, the nannies brought in a very pink abominable snow-baby. They placed her in my arms and made quick, tearful exits. She did not make a sound, but stared at me with big brown eyes. I took off one layer of clothes and offered a bottle of water. No drinking. More staring. More paperwork. Pictures of her staring. Silent. So we returned to the hotel. We had our little girl. She had lost the only home, family, and language she had ever known. She gained parents who focused on her every move and sound yet who were as unsure of being parents as they were about Chinese driving practices for which her car seat was my lap. We returned to the hotel and immediately sent pictures and prayer requests to our friends and family.

We started with the basics: although thirteen months old, Katie ShangQing could not sit up because her foster mother had never put her down. We laid her and her blanket on the floor to practice sitting up. She fell over when I moved away and was very shy about looking at me or moving in my direction. Charles went alone to Walmart to get formula, diapers, and a few toys. While his solo foray into downtown Kunming impressed our guide, it did not impress Katie. We could not replace her foster mother or her nannies. Her shiny A-B-C stacking block, however, was her best thing. She broke the shiny B block in two days. Still, she barely drank anything for three days. We gave up on the cough tea that the nannies wanted her to finish in favor of getting her to drink. Anything. Still, she ate the "nudles" that her nannies said she liked so much. She shuddered when we gave her ice cream. The hotel manager offered us parenting tips because we were clearly out of our depths. Then, on the third day, she grabbed a spoon and banged it on the hotel's dining room table. She smiled. We laughed in relief.

Apart from the silent staring, however, we had none of the troubles other members of our travel group experienced with their newly adopted children. And we all skirted around the rude facts of our children's origins and the monies we had paid to make those children ours. Katie's story is hers alone, yet that story is like so many others. Passersby found Katie screaming on the grass next to a major pedestrian underpass in the middle of a February night, her umbilical cord still soft. And somewhere, very likely nearby, was a mother who loved her child so much that she chose to carry her to term rather than take advantage of state-provided abortion services. Yet that same mother wrapped her newborn in a blanket, set her on the grass, and walked away. Katie's heart shattered, so she cried the grieving cry of the helplessly alone. Despite their own loss, Katie's birth parents must have hoped that other pedestrians would hear her and take her to the police station five hundred feet away. Perhaps they watched and waited. We will likely never know.

As hoped for, pedestrians picked her up and turned her in to the police. The police took Katie to the hospital where nurses worked to raise her temperature, which had dropped to about ninety-four degrees. She stayed four days. She then moved again to the Children's Welfare Home, which for three months advertised in the newspaper her picture and the details of her "finding." No one responded. So, the matron of the home began the process of preparing Katie, now four months old, for adoption. Katie's initial exam had revealed a heart murmur, which qualified her for the "special needs" list and placement in a foster-care farming village where the home often placed special needs children. So far as we know, Katie lived with her foster mother for about eight months. Then, she returned to the orphanage for about a week until we arrived. Katie is one of the lucky ones. Many children arrive at the home in far worse condition than hers, with greater needs, and with slim probability of adoption. Still, nothing erases the fact that she had lost her birth family in a few hours and her foster mother some months later. Naturally, she regarded us with suspicion—would she stay with us permanently, or were we just another short stay?

While we were in China, Katie slept in our bed, but when we arrived "home," she chose her room as her place to sleep. She would play with us and eat and drink what we gave her. She learned to enjoy the bath, and finally, we washed her hair. She giggled when we played silly games and grinned from ear to ear when she discovered that she could walk around pushing her Kai-Lan car. Yet all the love we can and do lavish on her does not erase her losses. She had to decide to adopt us as much as we decided to adopt her.

Katie still works to process the loss of birth parents, foster family, and language. She pretended for a year that she did not understand any Chinese, although at bedtime she asked for "ohm" and "ush," childish corruptions of the Chinese words for "prayer" and "storytelling." Sometimes she still screams in her sleep from a place so dark that she wets her bed. When we finally wake her from that dark place, she sighs with relief that she is at home with mommy and daddy. And we know that she has adopted us as her mommy and daddy. She comes to us with her itches and scrapes. She knows that when we leave we will return. She begs for us to read her books and announces that she is ready for letters and numbers as part of her bedtime routine. She plays school with her monkeys and grandma. When she worries about us because we are sick or sad, she blows us kisses to make us better. We know that she loves us. We are in that fleeting, magical childhood space when mommy and daddy can remedy most ills with kisses and cuddles. But only once has she spontaneously told me that she loves me. When we query her, "Guess what?" she replies, "You love me." I've started teasing her by responding, "No, *you* love *me*." I don't usually get an answer, just a head turned toward a stuffed toy or a giggling noise, as if the truth of that statement were a little much to breathe aloud.

One day, she will also ask how she came to our family without coming out of Mommy's tummy. We will tell her the truth—that we wanted her before she was born, that we worked with agencies and governments to find her and to make her part of our family. She may even learn how much her adoption cost us. Perhaps she will imagine the cost her mother paid to lay her down on the grass next to a highly travelled pedestrian throughway, turn her back, and walk away. Will Katie think that we bought her? Did we?

In some ways, yes. Did we engage in the trafficking of a human being? Not illegally, but yes.

We bought her at a price. We moved her citizenship from one country to another. She had no choice. The knowledge that we paid for her is deeply uncomfortable, despite the fact that we were her best option and despite the fact that at least some of our fees support those children who will grow up in that children's home. These questions of social justice and human rights will not disappear, nor can we ignore them.

But there's yet a larger picture: as Christians, we also were bought with a price. We did not become part of God's family for free or on the cheap. God paid dearly to make us his sons and his daughters; our citizenship changed the moment that we returned to God the love that s/he has lavished on us. We had to agree to our Godly adoption just as Katie had to agree to take us as her parents.

Beloved by us as we are beloved, Katie has two parents, numerous uncles, aunties, and cousins, a doting grandmother, friends to play with, and two cats. She informs us that when she turns five, she will get a puppy, and when she grows up, she wants to be a veterinarian. As she matures, she will continue processing her—and our—adoption story. Threaded in that story will be love given freely, hopefully, from parents to a child they wanted and returned from that child to parents who gave her enough love to return it a bit and even to fear its loss. Eventually, she will realize that she fears needlessly. Our mutual adoption will not erase Katie's losses or ours. It will, however, give us the completeness we lacked, sweet laughter for each day, and priceless hope for our future. Together.

3

Found by Grace

FORREST INSLEE

> But he said to me, "My grace is sufficient for you, for my power is made perfect in weakness." Therefore I will boast all the more gladly about my weaknesses, so that Christ's power may rest on me.
>
> 2 CORINTHIANS 12:9

As I waited in the courtroom that muggy day in October ten years ago, I took slow, deep breaths, willing myself to be calm. My friends and coworkers, witnesses I had brought along in support of my petition to adopt, seemed equally tense as the judge sifted through papers, considering the testimonies that had been offered on my behalf. All was quiet but for the sounds of traffic coming through the open window. Even Kayra, the one-year-old child I was proposing to adopt, was uncharacteristically still as she stood on the hard wooden bench, leaning into me, her fingers absently stroking my beard—a comfort habit she had picked up when she was just a month old. In that moment I was keenly aware that my life—our life together—hung in the balance as our future was being decided by this judge in a foreign land.

Yet as critical as that moment was, the process leading up to it was in fact what God used to transform me—to break me, really—leaving me a different man when it was all over.

I was living in a predominantly Muslim country—a footloose single guy, doing community development and leadership training for emerging churches in Istanbul. One day, a couple of friends approached me out of the blue to tell me (in their language) that I was soon going to be a father. Thinking that I was mistranslating, I asked them to repeat themselves, this time in English. Yes, they said matter-of-factly, they had a friend who needed to find someone to adopt her baby. They had come to let me know that their friend had chosen me to be the adoptive father.

In a moment of inspired insanity, I said, "Yes. Of course."

As you can imagine, this was all a bit of a life-shock. It was true that I had wanted to adopt a child since high school. To the idealist in me, adoption had always seemed like the ultimate act of biblical justice and a radical way to express godly love through lived action. I had apparently mentioned all this to my Turkish friends at some point, and they had taken my ideals seriously—more seriously than I took them myself, to be honest. The child's mother apparently knew something about me and had seen me interact with other children in the community. That, along with the testimony of my friends that I was a decent guy, seemed enough to convince her that I should be the adoptive father of her unborn child.

So there I was, faced with the decision to jump off of a figurative cliff. And in that moment I knew in the deepest part of me that there *was* no other choice, really. So I jumped.

Later on, of course, I completely freaked out. Yet when I calmed down enough to hear God's perspective on the matter, I began to understand God's intentions more clearly: I knew in the deepest part of me that to embrace this opportunity to adopt would change me profoundly and irrevocably. In the choice to trust in God to make a way through what I knew would be uncharted and difficult territory, I would come to understand God (and life in the kingdom) in a profoundly new way. Through the adoption option, I was being offered a chance to take a risk on the grace of God, who can make all things possible.

Fortunately, this revelation—basically, that God's grace was sufficient—came *before* I learned about all the obstacles I would be facing in the adoption process. There I was, a single male, a foreigner, and an "infidel" living in a Muslim country. Technically, when I agreed to adopt this child, the laws of that country did not allow a single man to adopt, much less a *foreign* single man. Yet even as I learned that encouraging bit of news, I also learned that in just a few months' time a set of *new* laws would be on the books that would for the first time actually make it legally possible for a single foreigner to adopt. So I was to become in effect a test case for these new laws. But because my situation was such a strange and—for some—culturally unthinkable situation, I faced resistance—bureaucratic and social—all along the way once the adoption process began.

The greater, more difficult resistance to my efforts to adopt—and later, even to my parenting as a single man in general—came from the culture itself. The common wisdom in that context held that no man could (or would want to) function effectively as a parent without a woman taking primary responsibility for the child. My friends, neighbors, and coworkers in that cultural context didn't quite know what to make of my desire to be a father without a woman to hold it all together.

After the child was born, the law required that I keep her in my home for "fostering" during a trial period of one year; then I could apply for legal adoption. I took custody of her as soon as she was born; thereafter, the sight of a man with a newborn frequently evoked an overt rebuke from strangers, all of whom assumed I had no idea what I was doing! Sometimes when I would walk with her in the park, policemen would actually stop me, demanding to know where the child's mother was. In any case, knowing about this built-in suspicion of single male parenting, I made sure that the baby's nanny came to court on the day the judge heard my adoption case.

Don't get me wrong; I bore no ill will toward any of those who opposed my adoption of this little girl. Culture is culture, and people react according to their intrinsic worldviews. My point in sharing these stories, rather, is to emphasize the extent to which the cards were stacked against me when it came time, at the end of my fostering year, to approach the court for permission to adopt. As my first year with this little girl unfolded, I became more and more aware of the circumstances standing in the way of permanent custody—even as I grew ever deeper in love with her. I began to look at the looming court date at the end of that year as either the beginning or the end of my life; the stakes seemed that high in the terms of my heart.

When the day finally came, though, I had a strange sense of peace about it all. Even knowing that if the judge ruled against me he could take my daughter from me then and there, I still decided to take her with me to court rather than to leave her at home. In some ways this was for me the penultimate moment of risking on grace. If God really wanted me to risk my heart and fall in love with this child as I had, then surely (I reasoned) God could overcome any obstacles to the legal technicalities of the adoption process. In a deeper place still, though, I knew too that God's grace would make a way for me—and for her—if in the end the court decided against the adoption. As terrifying as that prospect was, I had nevertheless come to believe that God's grace was that extensive.

To make a long story short, in the end, my little girl laughed and smiled and hugged me through the whole court appearance; the judge awarded me custody without hesitation. Afterwards, in the courthouse hallway, my waiting friends laughed and cried and hugged each other, and all I had to say was "Yes. Of course." And in that moment, the emerging revelation of the God who is able to do any and all things took hold of my heart and mind for good.

When it comes to adoption, I realize my story is not a very common one. For example, I was not, like most adoptive parents, looking for the opportunity to adopt; rather, my adoptive child in a sense found me. At the same time, I adopted as a single man (and I am still single); while I know they are out there somewhere, I have yet actually to meet a single adoptive father. Still, I share with many adoptive parents this newfound experience of God's capacity to make a way when there is no way, and to make possible what is impossible.

What is more, my story is extremely uncommon (and unlikely) in light of Muslim values. In the Islamic world in general, there are widely divergent views about whether adoption is a good thing, so I can only comment on my understanding that emerged from that particular context. I can say with certainty, though, that there is generally a strong divergence between the Christian view of adoption and the Muslim one. Christianity, of course, values adoption and holds it up as a metaphor for the process by which we all might become children of God, taking on God's name, his identity, and the birthrights that come from belonging to our new family. Islam, on the other hand, has a more ambivalent view. One reason for this ambivalence is that certain verses in the Qur'an seem to discourage or even forbid adoption. Verse 33:4, for example, reads, "God did not make your adopted son as your own sons. To declare them so is your empty claim. God's word is righteous and constitutes true guidance." While caring for and even fostering orphans within one's family could be seen as good and right according to the traditions of Islam, what is truly important is the purity of bloodlines: most Muslims contend that orphans may not assume a family name that is not theirs by blood. (Ironically, before the adoption, my daughter's surname was Özkan, meaning "true blood" or "blood of the family.")

I first encountered this aspect of the Muslim worldview in my work with "street boys"—kids who lived on the street, usually because they had been abandoned or rejected by their families. I heard countless stories from these boys about being rejected by a stepfather after their mother's remarriage; after all, it was explained to me, they were not of the new father's "blood" or true family lineage, and so he was not truly responsible to raise them as his own. As it was explained to me, there is a great emphasis placed on this notion of "blood relation" (or "kan," in the language of that country). For this reason, even if orphans might be cared for by the state or by extended family systems, adoption really isn't a common practice in countries with a strong Muslim influence. Indeed, in Turkey it was commonly accepted that if a child ended up in an orphanage, that child would remain in the orphanage until reaching adulthood.

So while I never said so overtly, it was understood by many in my church community there that by giving my name to my daughter, I was living out the principle of adoption inherent in the gospel and enacting a story of the grace God offers to all. It is, of course, a story of grace that continues to unfold today. We eventually moved back to the United States; I am now a university professor, and my daughter is about to enter middle school. And as I look back on the last ten years, I can see that my adoption and subsequent parenting have fundamentally changed me. While I tend now to think more carefully about the implications of my actions for parenting (I decided, for instance, against moving to Uganda when my daughter was sixteen months old—a little too scary), I *have* become fundamentally more of a risk-taker. I have, for example, developed a reputation among my friends and colleagues as someone who will willingly take action in the face of adverse circumstances. I've become one who urges others—especially my graduate students—to do the same. And when it comes to new projects and programs and ministries, I am quick to act out of the near-maniacal belief that if God is behind it, I merely have to walk forward to see any new endeavor come to be.

I teach in graduate programs for students on trajectories for the helping professions. Many of them tend to be idealists, with big dreams to change the world and pursue justice for the poor and the oppressed.

For their own good, I often have them read about the lives of people like Paul Farmer, who has essentially given himself to the poor and suffering of the world at great personal cost. My hope is always that my students will acknowledge the inspirational power in the way such "heroes of *shalom*" gave of themselves and their abilities for the cause of the poor, but at the same time recognize in themselves the fears, the limitations, the lack of zeal when it comes actually to following these examples of radical living. As shalom-bringers and potential world-changers, this is what they must confront before they can be any good to the world, or to the work of God's kingdom—this tension between what they know is good and right, and what they are actually capable of.

Of course, as Christians we are all called to live lives of radical shalom, and we must all confront that same tension. In sorting that out, however, maybe it is not so important that we figure out what we are *able* to do, but rather what we are actually *called* by God to do. I have become convinced that when it comes to the particular challenges involved with *the things God has given us to do* (as opposed to good works in general), God gives us great capacities far beyond ourselves. In that sense, it all comes down to having the courage to listen and to apprehend our true calling—and then to step out in obedience in the belief that God will both make us able beyond our innate abilities *and* give us the courage, zeal, and joy that comes only when we are truly living as an expression of true calling.

Don't get me wrong. In some respects I am still insecure when it comes to my parenting. I am, for example, afraid to talk to my daughter in detail about her birth father. For some reason, she has never asked about him—perhaps out of a sense of responsibility to protect my heart when such a discussion occurs? Or is it simply that she can't get her head around the idea of any other father but me. (I hope it is the latter!) Regardless, I *will* need to talk about him some day, and to reveal the fact that he was not a good man.

I am also afraid (in general), of trying to parent my daughter in her teen years! (Her grandma has already taken her to buy her first bra, so *that* scary thing is taken care of.) But I sometimes worry: as a single man, how will I deal with all of the pressures and struggles that are particular to young girls coming of age? (Just today she asked me which boy-band poster would look best in her room—a first for me. It was all I could do to offer a measured, objective opinion.) With my characteristic lack of patience and love of order, how will I handle her inevitable tumult of adolescent emotions? In view of my own insecurities, how will I ever be able to handle her expressions of emerging independence?

I am afraid—of these things and more. But here's my point: because of the profound grace I have experienced in the first ten amazing years of single-father adoptive parenting, I have come to believe without any doubt that God will always, *always* make a way. God will make a way for me to be the father *and* mother she needs to grow up whole, confident, and able. And God *always* makes a way for my daughter when I am not serving her as the best parent I should be.

In this very moment of writing, and indeed every time I remember God's profound grace that has sustained my fatherhood, my heart breaks at the reminder of God's mercy. Indeed, I am reminded every time I say her name: on the day my daughter was born, in a moment of prescience I suppose, I named her Kayra—which, in the language of her homeland, is the word meaning "grace, favor, and kindness." The grace of God that I've experienced in this process of becoming an adoptive parent has broken me wide open. It has shown me the depth of my incapacity for this thing called parenthood—and has shown me the limitless capacity of *my* heavenly parent's love and provision. Since this child came into my life, so much of the time I feel overwhelmed, even ashamed—not just of my lack of parenting skill but also of how truly unlike Christ I really can be. What adoption has shown me, though, is that God loves me enough to be absolutely and overwhelmingly present through all my weakness, for my sake and for the sake of my little girl.

4

When Adoption, Colorado Ranches, and *Kung Fu Panda* Collide

JEREMY COOK

"Progressive revelation" is the term my wife and I use to describe how we have told our adopted twin children their story. The revelation began by simply celebrating Homecoming Day—the day we brought them home from New Life Home in Nairobi, Kenya, when they were five months old. To them it must have felt like a birthday or Christmas, with gifts, special food, and even more hugs and kisses from Mom and Dad. When they reached video-watching age, we showed them a home video that includes scenes from their hometown, the hospital where they were born, the first orphanage that took them in, and our first month together as a family.

When they were almost four years old we spent a month in Nairobi, including a special afternoon at New Life Home, showing them around and playing with the babies there. We could tell by their faces that they were processing this experience in a profound way. On this trip they also began a friendship with a Kenyan girl who lived in Nairobi with her adoptive American mother. That friendship continues to this day as a meaningful relationship of shared experience, even if they do not yet understand it as such. On their fourth Homecoming Day we presented them with darker-skinned (and not easy to find!) Cabbage Patch Dolls and conducted little adoption ceremonies with certificates and all. Callie and Louie still share their beds.

The Spirit of Adoption

Today, their ninth Homecoming Day, progressive revelation involved reading excerpts from a new photobook of their early days that my wife put together. In it she included our email to friends and family the day we were matched with them and excerpts from a recent sermon of mine on the biblical doctrine of adoption. A few years ago, when we thought the time was right, we carefully explained that another woman gave birth to them, but for unknown reasons walked out of the hospital the day after their birth. Today for the first time they heard me read the word *abandoned*. It's not that the word is unfamiliar; they clearly know what it means. But it was the first time they heard that word in the telling of their story. And so today was the first time we cried together over this story.

Even now as I write, I wonder, did we err in using the word? Was it too early for their nine-year-old minds and hearts? We have never felt an ounce of anger or condemnation toward their birth mother. In fact, our overriding sentiment toward her is gratitude for having given birth to them in a hospital, let alone given birth at all. But the word *abandoned* is simply the best descriptor of what happened. Truly, they were abandoned. To describe it any other way would be to gloss over the pain they will continue to feel and wrestle with for perhaps the rest of their lives. And we can only imagine the pain their birth mother still feels, if indeed she is still living. We follow my mother's lead in praying for her, especially on their birthday. But in one sense it is much easier for us, for we have never felt the pangs of abandonment. Even as the progressive revelation and ensuing self-awareness unfolds, how do we help our kids wrestle with questions of abandonment? Any feelings of sadness or anger will be normal, perhaps even necessary, as they process their story. But today as I read them excerpts from my sermon on adoption, we observed a glimmer of understanding that in some mysterious way, their story, even their birth mother's story, has been caught up in a much greater Story.

Almost ten years ago now, the tragic plight of children orphaned by HIV and AIDS, particularly in Africa, captured my wife's heart and my heart. A visiting preacher at our church in Washington DC, told of his son's work in Zambia among orphans, where in that country alone orphans numbered in the hundreds of thousands. Figures for the entire continent, we learned, were mind-numbing. Yet at the same we were sensitive to how our own Western hearts and minds might process this information. That Sunday fell during a summer urban program that my wife and I had founded and had been leading for a few years. We were there with our twelve college students, with whom for several weeks we had been discussing issues of racism, privilege, poverty, and justice through the lens of the gospel of Jesus Christ. We had imitated as best we knew the Christian community development model of John Perkins and relocated to the neighborhood where we would invite these students to immerse themselves. We tried simply to be good neighbors as part of a tiny minority in that area of DC. We were not only aware of the "white savior" complex, but we actively searched our hearts for it and taught our students about it. Ten years later it is hard to know how much I'm looking back at us through rose-colored glasses. Were we naïve? Were we covering our naïveté with a veneer of enlightenment? After all, we were teaching on this, so *certainly* it wouldn't affect *us*. But the fact is I look back at us ten years ago, not with a rock-solid certainty, but with enduring confidence in the small decisions we began making that day.

In an almost crude way, our initial approach to adoption was partly pragmatic. Indeed, the genuine need of real children without a home, and the lack of parents to meet that need, took hold in our hearts. Yet we knew that we would move to Kenya in a few months, and we were quickly approaching the time in our marriage when we wanted to start having children. And here the grand arc of God's sovereignty appears to hover over our entire story, which I'll also describe in more detail later. Suffice it to say that on that Sunday afternoon we had planned a conversation about starting a family. We had no idea of the sermon topic, let alone any mention of orphans. That afternoon we took up more seriously than ever the topic of adoption. Whatever challenges we might face having biological children, we decided that it made sense to start with adoption because we were moving to Kenya primarily for my wife's job. Our general line of thinking went something like this: pregnancy may come at some point, but why not start first with adoption? So as we tell people now—because we get this question a lot—yes, before we moved to Africa we knew we wanted to adopt. We were ready.

Our unsentimental readiness served us well in those early days in Kenya. We felt patient and, for awhile at least, didn't think much about adoption. The details aren't important here, but initially Kenya was supposed to be a short-term training assignment for my wife before we moved elsewhere in Africa. So we knew that wherever we ended up in the long term, we would then seek to adopt. But weeks turned into months in Kenya, and the next step was not apparent. Before leaving the States I had been told by a family friend of a private orphanage with a strong reputation that was affiliated with Mission of Mercy (now One Child Matters). For several months I put off visiting, partly because I lacked the time but also because I didn't want to get attached to any children if we weren't able to stay in Kenya. We did not want to become attached to a child and fall prey to any notion that we had to rescue this child out of a bad situation and into our mostly good situation. But at some point I decided to visit New Life Home, partly out of self-conscious obligation and partly because I had some extra time on my hands. I thought I might be able to volunteer and do some good. I also love babies, so that was a bonus. And I didn't know if this orphanage even did adoptions, so I considered myself "safe." Little did I know that as soon as one crosses the threshold of this orphanage, one is greeted by a picture-laden poster that reads, "I need a Mum and Dad. How about you?"

In the history of orphanages, it is likely that few have ever fallen in love with an orphanage. But that day I did. Before I ever laid eyes on any of the orphans there, I sensed that this was indeed a place where anyone would want to adopt. The director of the home, a British missionary who with his wife had founded the institution less than ten years before, greeted me promptly. I didn't need long with him to know that New Life Home had been steeped in prayer. He told me their story. I told him our story, part of which was that in our approach to adoption we had become convinced that we wanted to adopt two children. Before moving to Kenya, our self-imposed homework assignment had included a book on transracial adoption.

Through reading the adult narratives of several transracially adopted people, we became convinced that we needed to adopt two so that each child had someone else in the family who looked different than Mom and Dad and with whom they could process questions of identity. As I shared this conviction, the director of the orphanage responded, "Well, we have twins!" Interesting, I thought. Duly noted. We wrapped up our conversation, and he had one of the employees give me a tour of the immaculate facility, including the nursery where twenty or so infants were taking their mid-morning nap. I don't know if she pointed out the twins or if I asked where they were. Honestly, I can't recall. But there they were sleeping in cribs next to each other in the middle of the room. Ketran was wearing Air Jordan sneakers. How could I forget that?

I left the place convinced that I would merely volunteer, but in reality I was a goner. Perhaps hindsight makes a fuzzy memory clearer, but the evidence is in an email I wrote that night to my wife, who was traveling in Sierra Leone. I laid out the details—including the twins—with enough passion that she broached the topic of adoption with her supervisor, who also happened to be on the trip. To make a long story short, because the move to another location in Africa had become delayed, she essentially got permission to stay and work in Nairobi even though the natural next step would have been to return to DC. We found that in many ways it takes a village to complete an adoption, including villagers we know as colleagues!

Shortly thereafter we were matched with Kayla Asali and Ketran Mjumbe. After receiving clearance from New Life Home's social worker, being matched simply meant being asked, "Would you like to see a list of the availables?" This question felt surreal, yet it made sense. There were those babies who needed a home now and were ready to leave. And we had decided that we wanted to offer a home to Kayla and Ketran, which of course the orphanage directors knew. But they followed standard procedure, asked the question, and we gave our answer, at which point they opened up the files and told us what they knew about their young lives. This revelation included the fact that both twins had twice tested negative for HIV. We were relieved, mostly for the kids' sake, but frankly because we also weren't sure at the time if we had what it takes to raise a child living with HIV. If the test results had been positive, we knew we would have to process the news together and make a hard decision either way.

These strange new realities around adoption compelled me to think anew about the Christian faith. The whole idea of choosing someone in a helpless state has helped lead me to a more Reformed understanding of salvation. Far more than me choosing God, it is clearer each day that God has chosen me, regarding my "helpless estate, and hath shed his own blood for my soul," as Horatio Spafford wrote in his hymn "It Is Well with My Soul." But adoption helps round out the picture and further reveals the heart of God. As Trevor Burke writes in his book *Adopted into God's Family*, "To be declared righteous at the bar of God [the courtroom of God] is one thing; it is, however, quite another to be adopted into God's family and able to call him '*Abba*, Father' (Gal 4:6; Rom 8:15)."[1] The Apostle Paul explains in a letter to his Roman friends that those who have received this gift of adoption experience the Spirit of God testifying with our spirit that we are children of God. This spiritual truth is reflected in my earthly experience of adoption, when I shuffle toward the coffee pot in the morning, greet my kids, and they respond, "Morning, Daddy." They don't need to run downstairs to the filing cabinet to check the legal adoption papers to know how to address me. I'm their *Daddy*! They know it in their guts; they know it in

---

1. Burke, *Adopted into God's Family*, 25.

their spirits. At five months of age they seemed to know in their spirit that they were part of a family.

A few weeks after being matched with Ketran and Kayla we were able to bring them home to begin the three-month foster period. Two weeks after Homecoming Day we took them back to the orphanage for a scheduled medical check-up. At first they wouldn't go back to the nurses who had raised them for five months. There was no going back, which certainly raised the emotional stakes as we approached the legal process.

In many ways the Kenyan adoption process in 2004 was straightforward and brief. American friends who adopted domestically or from China or Russia are astounded to learn that it took us only eight months. Of course, it doesn't feel that short while you're in the midst of the process. Plus, because we took the kids into our home as foster parents and underwent home studies before starting the court process, it was emotionally draining. We were completely smitten and couldn't imagine ever having to give them up. So naturally we approached the court process with a bit of trepidation, despite the confidence of our attorney.

One of the funny things about adopting in Kenya as a U.S. citizen is that you're not quite used to how Kenyans, having inherited the British system, address their judges. So our fantastic Kenyan adoption lawyer, who was used to having U.S. clients, prepped us on how to address the judge. You call him either "My Lord" or "Your Lordship." I thought I would pass on "My Lord," lest I picture myself talking to Darth Vader or Voldemort and crack up in the judge's chambers. I doubt that would have gone over well with our stern judge, who, thankfully, because he was not on the bench but only in his office, was not wearing one of the ridiculous white wigs that Kenyan judges still wear as a carryover from the British. But I digress.

Tamara and I were surprised to learn in advance that one of the questions His Lordship would ask us was, would these children have the same inheritance rights as any biological children you may have in the future? And indeed, he did ask us that. Well, I couldn't help myself here. Our file told him I was a missionary of sorts, and I just couldn't hold back. I told him that as Christians we understood ourselves to be adopted by God and thus had the full rights of sonship[2] along with Christ. Thus we could not possibly consider giving Ketran and Kayla less than full inheritance rights.

2. Paul's use of the masculine "sonship" in his New Testament letters is actually an expression of inclusivity, not exclusivity. His original Greco-Roman audience would have known only legal inheritance rights for sons. But now, through the gospel of Christ, both male and female would have the full rights of spiritual inheritance. Better yet, all of God's adopted children actually become coheirs with *the* Son of God.

He just stared at me blankly. But apparently that satisfied him because a few months later he signed the adoption decree. Now, over eight years later, God has blessed us with a biological child, but our wills remain the same. In fact, Ketran and Kayla's names are on the will, with only a few sentences stating that any future children will share equally in the estate.

If I could have sat down with that judge over a cup of hot Kenyan tea, I may have been tempted to tell of the grand arc of God's sovereignty that covers our story. A few weeks before our departure to Kenya, I spent a few days in orientation for InterVarsity Christian Fellowship staff who would be going overseas to work with sister organizations. During our last session together we prayed for each other as a sort of commissioning for the work ahead. I had shared with these new friends and colleagues our desire to adopt. When my turn came they gathered around me, and amidst other prayers, my supervisor, Becky, prayed for our children. I broke down weeping. I recall being surprised at my own reaction. After all, we had yet to identify an orphanage, let alone any children. It was just that sometime in the future we wanted to adopt. But something came over me that day at Bear Trap Ranch in Colorado.

Months later, after Ketran and Kayla came home to live with us, I broke down again. One day I had put them down for a nap and opened the computer. While looking at my calendar software, I noticed something that sent me convulsing in sobs. The very day that Becky prayed for our children was the very day that their birth mother abandoned them in the hospital.

Every so often I find that I have to go back to that story. Sadly, most days parenthood is about struggling with impatience over messy rooms, forgotten homework, and sibling drama. On those days I wish I could more easily bring to mind the greater drama in which we're all caught up. As the answer to Becky's prayer indicates, Someone is not only watching but also moving and shaking constantly. In the midst of what we plan to reveal progressively, surprises can crop up—even in the form of *Kung Fu Panda*.

About a year ago we decided on a whim to go see *Kung Fu Panda 2*. As is too often the case, it turned out to be a rainy day in Seattle, so retreating to a movie theater seemed like a good idea. We try to catch most animated films, especially if characters voiced by Jack Black help entertain us adults. We had no idea what we were in for. In the first *Kung Fu Panda*, parts of the story allude to Panda's adoption by, er, a goose, but it's a fairly minor part of the story. In the second installment, the adoption *is* the story. About a third of the way into the film, my wife and I gave each other the look that says, "Oh boy, here we go."

The Spirit of Adoption

Part of me wanted to ask the guy in the booth to pause the film at appropriate times so we could debrief as a family. It was actually quite intense. As I remember it, Panda has flashbacks to his abandonment due to an attack on his family. He questions his identity throughout the film. And then (spoiler alert!) at the very end of the film, we learn that his birth father is still living and then, THE END. No doubt, *Kung Fu Panda 3* is not far behind.

But we did not spend the car ride home imagining how the next film would unfold. Rather, we attempted to debrief. My wife and I probed with a few questions and then mostly tried to juggle the brief responses that we got. Debriefing for Ketran and Kayla would not be so easy. In times like those I have found myself wondering, "Aw, is it even that big of a deal? Aren't they just glad to have a loving home? Don't they actually care more about skateboards, soccer, and friends at school?" But then the floodgates open, and the deep things emerge. That night was the first night both of them cried over their story. One of them just wanted to know what *she* looked like. The other was concerned that something violent had likewise happened in their story. With both surprise conversations like these and our planned revelations, part of the difficulty is that we just don't know a lot of details. So we reiterated what we know and tried to honor their birth mother. (As a quick aside here, we know even less about their biological father, whose adjective I'll maintain since we don't even know if he was present at the birth. It wasn't until my wife had the first conversation with our daughter about sex that she realized she also has a biological father. I'm sure this in itself will lead to lots of unpacking in future years.)

So on that night and tonight, pain is revealed. Pain is not the only thing revealed, of course. But I wonder if in some strange way we honor their birth mother by acknowledging the pain. As deep as the joy is from our adoption, this is not some fairy tale. She lost profoundly, and we have gained immensely. We also face the highs and lows of adoptive parenthood, including the uncharted waters of adoptee identity formation into which we have not yet sunk. Whatever form of release she felt from walking away, she was never able to know what happened to them. Maybe one day she will, even if not in this life. My enduring hope for her is that she, in her helpless estate like mine, has been found by God and will join me in that great Homecoming Day. There will no longer be any pain to reveal, and it will all fade away as we sing about the pain experienced in nail-scarred hands and feet. That is the story I want our kids to go on singing about for eternity.

5

How Adoption Brought Me from Darkness to Light

MAGGIE LALICH

I am always amazed when neighbors, family members, and even strangers say how lucky my children are. It is obvious that my children are adopted. I am blonde, blue-eyed, and have fair skin. My beautiful children have dark hair, tanned skin, and brown eyes. My children are happy children.

When people say how lucky my children are, I want just to shout, to rejoice, and to respond, "*I am the lucky one!*" If they only knew me before, they would probably pity me and see an empty soul. The fact is my children saved me from a murky darkness of loneliness and lack of purpose. Their presence in my life brought me *back* to God. Through divine intervention and guidance, my destiny of motherhood was fulfilled.

In my late twenties I read books by Elisabeth Kübler-Ross and others regarding the existence of only two emotions: love and fear. Every thought and action evolved from these emotions. There was not a fight of good versus evil, but rather a choice of *coming to* love or *leaving* love. While experiencing love, you are more in the light, being positive, centered, and balanced. When caught in a place of fear, you move further away from the light, experiencing negativity, envy, incompleteness, and loss. At least this was my understanding. Being a Christian, I believed the light represented the love of Christ and one's spiritual being. I viewed my world differently from that point on. I did not see sin as simply originating with the devil, but rather as my personal choices affecting my emotions. When things were not positive in my life, I would try to figure out how to get back in the light, to be centered, and to be a part of God's love. Many times, I believe God called me back to the light.

Motherhood was always my greatest wish in life, so I tried to conceive a child with my husband. I was once pregnant. There was initially a heartbeat. But it was very short-lived, as the pregnancy was ectopic. Then I was whisked away for an emergency procedure. Darkness began. I tried to stay positive. I got pregnant once, and I believed it would happen again. I tried numerous expensive procedures, including hormone treatment, the administration of strong medicines, tracking down various medicines from numerous pharmacies, all to no avail. I lost the light, and my path became a treacherous downward slope. I prayed. I begged. I pleaded with my higher power. I fought with God. Try to understand—my mother had eleven children, but I could not bear any. I did not use drugs or alcohol. Many of my friends who engaged in these activities in early adulthood conceived beautiful children of their own. I was shrouded with envy for all mothers. Descending into a deeper darkness, I believed that I had failed my husband. I could not give him a child. I lost confidence in who I was meant to be. In the middle of it all, friends and colleagues were having babies, showers, and celebrating Mother's Day. Artificial insemination worked for everyone else, so why didn't it work for me? I started hating the world. I cried at work and hid away. I cried at home and sat in my living room during many sleepless nights. I wondered why God gave me this desire to be a mother, to want children, yet I was unable to conceive. Maybe there really wasn't a God. I wondered, "Why doesn't my husband just divorce me and find a woman who could give him children?" I blamed myself, believing that our inability to have a child must be my fault. The pain was emotional and physical. "What is the purpose?" I asked. My faith was shaken.

I could not hide from children: I am a teacher. At school I had children who loved me and wanted to come home with me. Most of my students' parents were wonderful. But I also met some parents who did not appreciate the gift that they were given. I knew children who were starved for affection and attention. Where was the justice? I prayed to Ruth and the Virgin Mary to help me. My prayers were not answered. Discouraged, I began hating God, my life, even the blessings I did have. I left the light and figured that there was no God or that my God had abandoned me. What was my purpose? Once again, hiding and crying, I did not know what to do. The weight was drowning me. I knew that I would not go in for another procedure, as I could not endure further empty results.

At rock bottom, I had often heard, a spark of light will come. That spark of light was my good friend Dana. "Why don't you go to that adoption agency down the street," she suggested. "You are meant to be a mom!" My husband was ready for some hope, too. That night, we went to the adoption agency office after hours, just to locate it. The light in the office was on. Some kind people invited us to sit and talk, which we did—for two hours. Instead of more fear, hope began to grow within me. After completing a *lot* of paperwork proving that we would make wonderful parents, waiting for a picture of our child, and then a long plane ride, I held a beautiful baby in my arms. Within twenty-four hours, my darling little girl and I had bonded. Samantha would not let me out of her sight. Others saw it, too! I was glowing in the light. I was saved. I had purpose, and I could begin loving fully again. What a lucky girl? No, what a lucky mommy! I thanked God for that perfect fit of daughter and mother. We were meant for each other. My family was together and happy. Samantha was meant for us.

I realized that God did not abandon me. There was a plan in my life; I just did not know the details of the journey. I had a destiny and so did my daughter. I would become a mother, but through adoption. Samantha would belong to a wonderful family who would love her. Years later when my daughter started kindergarten, I realized that Samantha was the same age as the child that we lost.

Of course, our family life was everything we had hoped! We loved Samantha with all of our hearts. And we decided we wanted another child, this time a boy. It was destiny, but once again it would happen in God's time. The Chinese adoption program had slowed down. Policies had changed. It took two years for our daughter, but it would be four years for our son.

In 2009, we were at Disneyworld with our daughter, enjoying our vacation. We were riding a bus to one of the parks when my husband looked at me. "I don't think that we can wait any longer," he said. "It's time we changed to another adoption agency that places children with special needs." I agreed. Five minutes later, my husband received an email inquiring if we wanted to move to a new special needs program that our current agency was opening. We knew God was listening to us. A few days later, we got a call from the agency; we were told not to worry about paperwork and that they would move us to the special needs list. I let them know that we wanted a boy. Two days later, we were given pictures of three boys. After almost four years of no progress, we suddenly found ourselves on a roller coaster ride.

We decided on a lovely boy about eighteen months old with a heart murmur. Henry (the name we gave him) was from the same region as Samantha. Then the race began. We had to update our information, especially mine. As with all surgeries, my ectopic pregnancy surgery was questioned. I needed to find a doctor who would write a letter stating that this surgery would not impact my life span. I needed this documentation, or we would have to forfeit the child. My doctor was out of town. The doctor who performed my surgery was no longer in the Houston area. My current gynecologist would not see me. I sat for hours in her office, waiting for a chance to try to talk to her. Finally, she stated she would not write a letter approving a procedure performed by another doctor. I was devastated. She had been my doctor for ten years. She knew of my struggle to get pregnant. I was shocked and felt completely abandoned. This ectopic pregnancy was still haunting me. It was out of my control. Darkness crept in; I felt as if I couldn't breathe. I wondered if God was testing me, trying to see how hard I would work for another child. Why was I being tested? I wanted this child. I called my husband in a panic. I was running around desperately trying to keep this child from slipping through my hands. We had a forty-eight-hour window. At the last hour, another doctor in my general practitioner's office saw me. Seeing the extent of my anxiety, she agreed to write a general letter stating that I was in good health and that the procedure would not shorten my life span. A beacon of light shone. The letter was mailed immediately and our adoption was approved. Needless to say, our son, Henry, has been worth every tear and ounce of frustration with the adoption process.

When we flew to China to adopt Henry, a wonderful surprise awaited us in the form of another chance meeting. The women who brought Henry to us began asking questions about Samantha. We told them Samantha was from the same region and the women realized that they had cared for Samantha years earlier. We told them Samantha's Chinese name, and the women recognized it. They told us that there was a picture of Samantha in their office that had been sent to them years ago. I knew exactly which picture it was, as I knew the family in our organization who had sent it. I saw an amazing light in these women's eyes; their love and care of these little girls and boys was important and made a difference in so many lives. Seeing Samantha was special because these caregivers rarely get to see the children again. God's divine presence was in that room. Having an opportunity to thank them for caring for our children was a blessing to me. I will never forget that precious moment.

God has allowed me to help others out of their own darkness to find the light in adoption. A friend and colleague, Holly, was struggling with the inability to have children. I recognized her anguish, envy, and pain. We talked almost daily. Holly was able to witness my life with Samantha. I reminded her that adoption was a way to begin a family and heal wounds. A parent does not have to be biologically connected in order to love, nurture, and care for a child. That person just has to want to love and care for the child. When that chosen child is placed in the new parent's arms, all the darkness begins to fade and the love of family begins to flourish. I am proud to say that Holly adopted two wonderful boys through a domestic agency and is the happiest homemaker anyone has ever met. Due to adoption and her first son's extreme food allergies, she has now become an advocate for increasing awareness of food allergies in children and has helped raise money to fund scientific studies.

Adoption deepened my faith when it was disturbed. I do believe in God's divine purpose more than ever. I know that if I had not adopted, I would not be the person I am today. I was meant to be a mother, and adoption gave me that opportunity. God had a purpose for my children, my husband, and me. I strive to live in the life and grace of God. The journey is not always what I might plan exactly, but it is what God's will means for me to experience and to learn.

6

The Right Fit?

ELIZABETH HUSTON

My adoption story started early. I was adopted locally at ten days old, by parents who had been trying for ten years to have children. The parents who raised me were relatively well-to-do. Not rich, but we always had a roof over our heads, nutritious food on the table, and activities outside of school to occupy us. I do not remember the day they told me I was adopted because they told me many times in small ways over the course of years. Although they never kept it a secret from my sister and me, their philosophy was to tell us only the basics until we asked for more information. I could not put words to it then, but something deeper was missing, even though up until a few years ago I would have denied it.

My birth parents were not married and did not continue to have a relationship after my adoption. I later learned that my birth mother, fearing that her parents would force her into an abortion, kept her pregnancy a secret. She carried the pregnancy very small and was able to hide it under sweatshirts for months. The truth came out about eight months into the pregnancy, and with it came the anticipated argument about the necessity of an abortion. Unluckily for her parents, that heated argument led to stress labor for my birth mother, and I was born that night. Adoption was not the first course of action for my biological grandmother. First, she dragged my birth mother to my birth father's house and proceeded to berate him in front of her, demanding that he marry her. He did propose, I am told, but my birth mother refused. Only then did adoption enter the picture, and my birth mother agreed—knowing all too well, perhaps, what life for me would mean with such grandparents.

Depression, self-loathing, and anxiety were recurring features of my childhood. For years, I attributed these issues solely to bullies at school and the typical trials and tribulations of growing up. I defended adoption as the best and only option in unwanted pregnancies and encouraged pregnant friends who were considering it. When they fretted over what it would mean to their unborn children in later years, I told them that all I had needed to hear was that my birth mother had given me up out of love. Perhaps I even believed those assurances.

In the last few years, however, my eyes have been opened to the drawbacks of adoption. I have come to realize that my feelings of inadequacy, my lack of trust that loved ones will stay in my life if I am anything other than perfect, and my sense that I simply do not fit all stem from my having been adopted. The manner in which my parents have overlooked the effects of adoption on me as their child, in addition to their own separate issues, has only amplified my struggles. My parents were prepared for a child, not an *adopted* child.

My family never made adoption an issue in my childhood, yet in my own home I was distinctly *othered*—set apart and treated as if I were, on some level, fundamentally different. Consistent, regular reminders of my differences left me with the feeling that I could not be loved simply as I am. My family often pointed out the ways in which I was *weird* or *unlike* them. For example, after graduating from high school, my mother and I met my birth mother, who, my mother noticed, was prone to talking with her hands. Afterward, my mother confessed that my tendency to talk with my hands had always annoyed her, but now she could see where I had come by this behavior. That hurt me, and it still hurts me—not only because she disliked a behavior of mine of which I had been unaware and could not help, but also because she had highlighted another way in which she had been incapable of coming to terms with who I am.

I think my mother in particular went into the adoption wanting a child who was fully hers, thinking that getting a baby meant I would grow to be like her. As I grew less and less like her, however, she did not attempt to encourage or understand me. Even small features of my personality, like the ruthless childhood honesty that often led me to confess guilt or express sincere sentiments, were often met with distrust. She could not fathom an honest child, since it did not fit into her idea of a normal family, so my thoughts, feelings, and confessions were treated as highly suspect, which in turn led me to doubt the value of my own virtues over the years—a tendency I am only beginning to overcome.

I think my mother, and my family as a whole, could have helped me overcome many of the effects of adoption had they chosen not to other me. My differences challenged and possibly frightened them, and their response was to shame those differences out of me. As it was, I felt as though I could not share with them the pain of being bullied, both as an elementary school student and, later, as a junior higher. The sense of not fitting in anywhere, which was perpetuated by my family, made it extremely difficult not to internalize the ostracizing actions of other kids. When I switched schools in first grade, I was shunned for "being weird." The popular kids in my first/second grade split classroom made it clear that anyone who wanted to be *their* friend would not become mine. Later, there were two girls with whom I desperately wanted to be friends but who truly wanted to be friends only with each other. They frequently came up with reasons (whether real or imagined) why they couldn't be my friend anymore, only to take me back a week later. I was so desperate to fit in with someone, I remember sobbing and begging them to be my friend again; they would turn to me and say, "What's the big deal? We'll forgive you again next week."

My sense of not belonging continued into junior high, and my need to fit in drove me to accept behaviors that even my most "cool" peers found unacceptable. After a P.E. class in junior high, a friend of mine, who struggled with pain issues and would occasionally lash out as a result, berated me for something. An entire locker room full of girls—who were not my friends and had never acted as though they cared for me much—threatened her with violence if she didn't stop the cruelty. My response to them was to beg them, sobbing, not to hurt her.

For a long time, I did not connect my struggles in interpersonal relationships with the subtle rejections of my childhood. But now, from my vantage point as a post-college adult who has begun to work through these issues, I recognize that many of the pieces of my life and self that did not fit are connected to my adoption. My experiences in school, and my ongoing experiences as an adult, have shown me that although I have a family, adoption has not been a solely positive experience for me. In fact, in many ways, adoption left me more vulnerable and less resilient in childhood, which affects me to this day. I have come to accept that adoption leaves no one unscathed; it is not a perfect solution. Other options exist, and I now recognize that, for some, adoption may not be the best option.

7

Kiki

Kohleun Adamson

The sun shone through stained glass windows on both sides of the platform, shooting wide bands of red, blue, and orange across the room. That's where she stood—in the crossfire of windows blazing. Everybody knew who she was. She was the senior pastor's seventeen-year-old daughter, Kiki.

Children's church had just ended, and we were all ushered back from the basement to our parents for the last few minutes of the service. They had plucked me, with my red paper handiwork, from my tasty paste cup, to come back and sing with the adults. I held the beautiful creation to my nose and smelled its sweet, sweet paste as I peeked over the balcony railing and down towards the stage.

Kiki's hair was long and blond, falling straight down her back, sometimes catching her shoulder, and looking very lovely. She always had perfectly curled bangs, and I knew when I was her age that's exactly how I would style my hair. Kiki was the most beautiful grown-up girl I knew. She was crying that morning and the very tips of her wet bangs stuck to her face just below the eyebrows. I had never seen her like that. On nights when Stephanie, our usual babysitter, was busy, Kiki would watch my brother, sister, and me when Mom and Daddy went out. She made the best macaroni and cheese. I stood by the stovetop watching her stir in the orange powder, milk, and butter as the spoon made a funny sloshy sound, and we giggled.

But this day was different.

The Spirit of Adoption

Every few seconds, a big sniff came from behind the podium as she talked. I thought, *She's crying, and she'll have snot on her face.* But nobody brought Kiki a tissue.

I gripped the railing posts and stood on tiptoes, waiting for someone to hug her like my parents hugged me when I cried. After wiping her nose with the back of two fingers, Kiki said a few things I didn't understand, but when she got to the end, her words rang loud and clear: "I am very sorry. Please forgive me." Was she talking to Jesus? At the county fair that year I had learned from the Bible Story Lady that all we needed to do to go to heaven was ask Jesus to forgive us, and he'd take care of it. That must be who she was talking to. But then she said, "I lied to you all."

From the balcony, Kiki looked as small as the American Girl dolls in the catalogs by my sister's bed. Her parents waited in the first row, seated next to my dad, the associate pastor, and I didn't see Kiki's curly-haired boyfriend, Robbie, anywhere, even though I stretched my neck like a goose. I waited for a hymn to play, since that's what happened whenever people got up to talk about Jesus and cry. There was no music as Kiki stepped down the stairs, hugging her own arms.

The following Christmas, after Kiki started carrying around a cute baby boy, I sat in her parents' house, very close to the Christmas tree, while the grown-ups talked about being too fat and ate sugar cookies with not enough frosting. I counted how many presents were in green paper, and how many were in red, and imagined opening them one by one. I always wished that when people threw parties those gifts under the tree were for their guests, or at least for me.

Everybody's clothes looked nicer than what they wore on Sundays, some with what looked like tree tinsel woven right into their shirts. Probably thirty people came to that party, and they all knew *everything* about each other's lives. My older sister Kari whispered, "Robbie is coming," as if it were a dirty secret, pulling me from greedy daydreams. I sneaked a peek out the window and saw Robbie walk up to where Kiki stood, denim-clad, in the yard with their son in blankets and a little car cradle. The young parents wore cozy sweaters as they ran across the lawn, making faces at the baby and laughing. I wished I could go out and play with them—enjoy their happiness—but I stayed in the house, careful to not snag my sparkly Christmas dress.

∽ ∽ ∽

As I grew older I learned through a mixture of osmosis and intuition why Kiki had to ask for everyone's forgiveness, why she was crying, why the rumors flew around about her, and why her parents looked so pained that day and for a long time after. Why Kiki blew up like a balloon, why she had a son before she was married, why I felt things in the air I still can't name, why she stayed to herself during church functions after that lonely Sunday, and why we always heard whispers of that awkward, ugly phrase, "out of wedlock." Why each person who said it contorted her face a little as if the ugly words tasted like vinegar. As a kid, I had no idea what those words meant anyway, but it was bad, for sure bad. And I didn't want to be bad. After all, I'm a pastor's daughter too.

My parents have tried very hard to let us kids be real human beings, and not perfect display models. We never talk about Kiki, but we don't have to; there are always reminders that we lead a kiss-and-others-tell life. Pressures rise and fall at potlucks, and offhand comments—criticism or praise—reinforce proper "P.K." behavior. It's impossible to forget our role.

When my younger brother wanted to pierce his ears and add #14 gauges—which totally freaked even me out—Dad gave him a definite "No." Within an hour of my arrival from college Mom asked, "Kohleun, please tell Luke college women don't find earrings on guys attractive." I glanced between mother and son, both staring attentively, and answered plainly, "I don't think I can honestly say that."

As we piled into the minivan and headed to a family reunion near my grandparents' home in suburban Minnesota, Kari informed me: "Even though Mom and Dad really don't care about ear piercing, the church does, and what we do reflects on his ministry. Do you remember Kiki?" she asked.

How could I forget Kiki?

"Her pregnancy could have ruined Pastor Johnson's ministry. Even though it wasn't his action, the church held him responsible. And that's how people think of us."

I saw the diamonds on Kari's wedding ring glint in early August sunlight, and turned to my niece Amy, asleep in her car seat. Her little chest rose and fell in a mini pink T-shirt. I sat quietly, watching trees and lakes flash past the window, and nodded, as if all this was perfectly acceptable to me, too.

After summer's end and another semester of college, I went home.

The people who gather within the brick walls of my childhood church start asking about me weeks before my visits. While I am in town, they say how proud they are of me and how wonderful it is to have "Christian scholars" these days. And I know asking, "You're studying philosophy—you aren't learning how to hate God, are you?" is supposed to be in my best interest. What they don't know is that, to borrow Anne Lamott's honest words, I'm a "bad Christian." I'm one of those crazy feminist, antiwar, anti-homophobia, let's-listen-to-Palestinians Christians.

While home for a visit recently, I got to talking with a couple who have known me since I was nine. Somehow the conversation found its way to me *hypothetically* coming home pregnant, of all things. Because if we joke about stuff like that it won't happen. I guess.

"Yes, but we know you would never do that," the man said.

"Your daddy would spank you," the woman said.

They both laughed.

෴෴෴

I know very little about my own birth or the mother who birthed me. In a grey fireproof box, along with my birth certificate, naturalization papers, and Social Security card, is a sheet of folded paper, kept safe for me by the couple I know as Mom and Dad. On that page is the record of a young Korean mother: her height—an encouraging 5'6"—hometown, and marital status: single. My Korean father's information is also there in black typewriter ink, so I like to think of myself as a love child. It is always better than turning to the alternatives. I never imagine my Korean mother in her forties like my mind knows she is. Instead, she is forever a dark-haired Kiki. I picture her with curled bangs, telling her family in a language I do not speak that she is sorry. Her chin is dropped low, eyes downcast, and she's weaving her fingers through each other and ripping them apart again. But here is where my imagination stops. Did they shame her? Did they make her apologize to the whole community? Did she even have a family to tell?

෴෴෴

For the first eighteen years of my life I attended an evangelical Christian church every week. I've heard countless sermons on the leper who came back to thank Jesus, short Zacchaeus's famous tree-climbing adventure, and Saul's roadside conversion. After all this time, one Sunday has stayed in my memory—each detail still clear after so many years—but I have no recollection of which songs were sung or what sermon was given. I remember Kiki.

Mom and Dad tell me my Korean mom put me up for adoption because she couldn't take care of me; she wanted to give me a better life than she had to give, a better world than the one in which I was born. And I thank her for that. Sometimes I wonder: did she dream of the little girl who would sit in a balcony holding a red paper heart that read, "God loves Kohleun"? Did she know I would be watching, horrified, as a pastor's teenaged daughter stood alone to face people who often scared grown adults? Did she worry that someday I would view her as beneath me? I wish instead there were a way she could know that same girl would show me how brave the mother who gave me life was.

I continue to picture my birth mother as a seventeen-year-old with curled fringe falling across her forehead, when in reality she probably had hair as straight and wiry as mine. She was twenty-two, the same age I am now. Life experiences make it nearly impossible to see my Korean mother when I look in the mirror. I have a college degree; she had an eighth-grade education. I've traveled the world; she never left her hometown. She had a baby; I've never even been in love. But I think these differences make Kiki that much more significant in my story. I can now see myself as the baby growing in the belly of a brave young woman, and when I meet mothers in similar situations, compassion and respect swell in my heart.

If I were a "good," sparkly Christian, I would have to remember Kiki's confession as a lesson that my life is everyone else's to observe from padded pews. I would have to remember my Korean mother as a blot on my life story, and myself as a shameful confession.

But, thanks be to God, that is not what I remember.

8

On (Not) Fearing the Mystery of God

MELANIE SPRINGER MOCK

Just days before our trip to India, birthplace of my second son, a well-meaning relative cornered me at a family gathering.

"We'll be praying for you!" she said, uttering the Christian phrase that can be, at the same moment, both cliché-riddled and completely sincere.

I chose to interpret it as sincere, needing all kinds of prayer for our journey. My husband and I were flying to India with our then six-year-old sons: Benjamin, whom we'd adopted from Vietnam as an infant, and Samuel, whom we brought home from Mumbai as a three-year-old. This was no ordinary homeland trip. My adult stepdaughter was marrying an Indian, and we were traveling to her fiancé's family village high in the Himalayan foothills for the ceremony.

Anticipating the trip filled me with terror. I hated flying already, and a fifteen-hour plane ride with two active boys made me even more fearful. I thought about negotiating a busy city with easily distracted kids in tow. And about a seven-hour car ride to my son-in-law's home, the crazy Indian traffic, the lack of car seats.

I feared malaria and diphtheria. Infections. The Delhi Belly that had brought my husband low during our adoption trip to India several years earlier, and the pinkeye that had plagued me on the same trip. I worried about my sons' emotional wellbeing and about whether Samuel would wonder—or not—about his birth family and culture. I was anxious about how I might explain the abject poverty evident everywhere in India, and if

Samuel especially might connect the poor he saw to his own early life in an orphanage.

In other words, I worried about everything. I needed prayer.

So I cherished my relative's assurance that she would be praying. Until she provided a follow-up: "I'm afraid that the boys might get influenced by Hinduism during the wedding ceremony, so I'll pray that doesn't happen."

I smiled at her. Said nothing. Fumed.

"Are you kidding me?" I wanted to scream, but knew that doing so might mess with the uneasy equilibrium that characterized these family gatherings. I thought, "My kids will *die* in a fiery plane wreck, and you're worried that they might learn something new about another religion?"

Her comment didn't make sense to me. Even now, six years after returning from my stepdaughter's wedding in India, I remain baffled by her apparent fear that my kids might be defiled by a Hindu wedding ceremony. My sons became Christians only by virtue of their adoption into our home, and they might well have been Hindu or Buddhist had they remained with their first families. Would God really respond to a prayer asking that they be protected from knowledge of the religions into which they were born?

Embedded in my relative's comment is a significantly more problematic idea, one voiced by those who adopt with a missionary's zeal, certain that, save for adoption, children would not be saved from eternal damnation.

That, at least, is a theology to fear.

෴ ෴ ෴

My husband and I had adopted on a whim. Of sorts. After years of going back and forth about whether we wanted to have children, I decided the answer was yes: children it was. Watching twenty-four-hour television coverage of a terrorist attack and seeing the United States irrevocably changed by the Twin Towers' collapse can make you reevaluate your own life's meaning, and that's what happened. In my reevaluation, I found my life wanting for something more, and concluded—along with my husband—that having children was the more we needed.

A little too naively, perhaps, we believed that adopting might be a better path toward making a family than having biological children. My husband already had two older children, and I felt no strong urge to give birth; so we decided that, somehow, bringing several children into our home would symbolically at least reflect our longing for a reconciled world. Several of our friends had just started the adoption process for a special-needs boy in India, and we admired their dedication in carrying that child into their home. So we said yes to a family, and yes to adoption, and yes to finding a child (or children) who could make our home complete.

As we signed with an agency, assembled paperwork, and secured our spot on country waiting lists, we did so without considering the many moral and ethical complexities adoption raises. We thought, initially, that we were saving a child from a life of poverty. That was pretty cool for us, two parents who wanted to have a family but didn't feel any intense need to bear more biological offspring. We didn't think about the problems of removing a child from his birth land, or what it meant for us, as relatively wealthy Westerners, to enter a developing country, put down a large amount of money, and bring a child to the United States to live with a new family who could supply his every physical need.

And then some.

I also didn't consider how adoption would shape my understanding of paradox, held close and reconciled in the mysterious hand of God. Understanding the complexities of adoption and its many paradoxes would only come later, much later, after we brought Benjamin home from Vietnam in 2002, and Samuel home from India in 2005. While I am still grateful moment by moment that we decided to adopt these two children—even when they fight, relentlessly, over every little thing imaginable—I remain perplexed by how I am to reconcile the paradoxes adoption presents to me and, by extension, how I am to understand an inscrutable God.

About paradox? Here's what I mean:

As I've considered my life with Benjamin and Samuel, as we've grown into family together, I've recognized that the capacity of God's love is more a mystery to me than ever before. For while I rejoice in the providence of my children and their miraculous presence in my life, I know the gift of my children is premised on someone else's loss. My sons have lost the opportunity to grow up with their birth families in their own culture. And my sons' mothers, who gave up their children because poverty or illness or other life circumstances made it impossible to raise the children they bore, have lost the opportunity of watching their beautiful sons grow into adulthood.

We know only a little more about Samuel's birth family than we do Benjamin's: we know that Samuel's first mother was very ill, and that she relinquished her son to an orphanage when he was one week old. Of Benjamin's first mother we know nothing, except that her son was near death when he was born, weighing only three and a half pounds, and that she left him at a hospital for extensive care. Despite this lack of information, I am aware—in general terms—of the conditions under which most women in developing countries must relinquish their children: they are poor and cannot adequately feed their children; or they are unwed and cannot resist traditional societal mores; or they are made ill by impoverished lives and will die before their children can be raised.

Because of this knowledge, and because I believe God is also compassionate, just, and merciful, I have struggled to understand this paradox: that for many adoptive parents, joy comes at great pain to others. As much as I love my children, I recognize that my position as a woman who is Western, white, and relatively wealthy affords me the blessing of motherhood, and that I can understand dimensions of God's nature—God's capacity to carry life and beauty and love to me—because I have been given a privilege my sons' birth mothers could not enjoy.

I also recognize the losses my own sons will feel, not knowing their first mothers, their first cultures, their first tongues. Because I love my children so fiercely, I am mourning their losses, long before they are capable of recognizing or acknowledging them. Still, I imagine the time may come when Benjamin and Samuel will wonder about their pasts, and I will not be able to give them the answers about their families that they seek, nor the assurances that all is well with those who carried and bore them.

Here too, then, is deep mystery, felt acutely by my sons in ways I never will. They carry with them the unfinished puzzle of their very origins, shaping their own relationship to an enigmatic God.

※ ※ ※

Do others who adopt consider this enigma? Sometimes I wonder.

For some people, the complexities of adoption, its paradoxes and mysteries, seem to matter little. In recent years, a number of evangelical churches have started "adoption ministries," compelled by the biblical mandate to help widows and orphans and certain that adopting is the best way to provide aid to the world's most vulnerable. Adoption becomes an evangelizing tool, allowing Christian families to save children physically but also—more significantly—spiritually, keeping them from the pits of hell. One proponent of this approach to adoption, Dan Cruver, author of *Reclaiming Adoption*, says this: "The ultimate purpose of human adoption by Christians, therefore, is not to give orphans parents, as important as that

The Spirit of Adoption

is. It is to place them in a Christian home that they might be positioned to receive the gospel."[1]

This evangelizing impulse of some Christians has always been problematic to me. The theological implications of the idea Cruver and many other evangelical adoption advocates espouse are astounding. If I follow this line of thinking to its conclusion, my own two sons would have burned in hell, save that they were adopted by white, wealthy Christians who could take them to church, have them baptized, raise them up as believers.

Those persons convinced that adoption saves children's souls seem to have a clear sense of who and what God is, a certainty I cannot fathom. They are certain that God redeems only those who have accepted the gospel. They are certain that a Christian is the best parent to a child. They are certain that adopting will assure that child's eternal life. (They are certain there *is* eternal life.) They are certain that God can work only through those with privilege and power, rather than through the least of these, no matter if they were born into a Hindu or Buddhist or Christian family.

They are certain a child, attending the Hindu wedding of his sister, will need protection from evil influences, lest his soul be lost forever.

꽃 꽃 꽃

My own prayers about our journey to India had been answered.

We didn't die in a fiery plane wreck, nor on the winding road to Garwhal, my son-in-law's familial home. On the way to Garwhal, my supplications were especially ardent. My sons rode without car seats. Large buses, trying to pass on narrow highways, came charging at our vehicle at speeds convincing me of our soon demise. Still, we survived. No malaria befell us, despite my sons' unwillingness to swallow the bitter antimalaria drugs we'd brought along. No diphtheria or Delhi Belly. No pinkeye. Our only casualties included a shirt, lost to me when my son barfed on it riding down a winding road, and an evening spent with a son, sleeping off a fast-moving bug, rather than celebrating with the wedding party.

The wedding itself took place on a cool evening, just as the sun was setting over the Indian plain. Our families gathered next to the temple, with Melissa and her new husband, her parents and his, sitting in a square around a fire pit. The priest, conversant in Hindi and in English, promised to narrate each step of the ceremony so that his American guests could understand the symbolism of each act.

---

1. Cruver, *Reclaiming Adoption*.

My boys and I sat just outside the circle, behind the bride and groom, until they, as the brothers of the bride, were called by the priest to give their sister away in marriage and to sanctify the bonds between her and her new spouse. And so they did: following the priest's directions to give rice to their sister each time she circled the fire, to wrap her hand with Rahul's, binding her forever to him. My sons also received a red dot on their heads, a tika which marked each boy as sacred.

I watched them, their smiles betraying the pride they felt at being called into the circle, into the ceremony. As my stepdaughter and her new husband rounded the fire once, twice, several more times, I was caught up in the ceremony's beauty and the power of being enfolded by Rahul and Melissa and the new family they'd created.

But mostly, I thought about my son Samuel, and about what might have been his fate had he remained in India. I imagined him circling the sacred fire, similar to the one my stepdaughter and her husband circled, celebrating his new family. I imagined him handsome in his kurta, his brilliant smile drawing everyone into his space, just as it does now. I imagined him as a Hindu, bowing faithfully to his own understanding of God. Except for adoption, he would probably have enacted these sacred rituals of his first family's faith tradition.

Now, he attends a Quaker church, goes to Sunday school, plays tag in the churchyard after services. One day, he will probably be married in a Christian church. There may be no kurta, no tika, no fire to circle. The sacred acts of his life have changed, one for another, because he has become a member of my family. Still, I believe the God to whom those acts are directed remains the same: beautiful, gracious, loving, merciful, divine.

And a mystery, nonetheless.

◠ ◠ ◠

Last year, our family traveled to Vietnam, to visit Benjamin's birthplace. Then as before, when we were preparing for our journey to India, I fretted about airline rides and sickness, drinking tainted water and getting malaria. I worried about crazy Vietnam traffic and about taking an overnight train through the countryside. I wondered how Benjamin would process what he saw, the homeland he couldn't remember. I prayed ardently and often that Benjamin would feel connected to Vietnam, that he would be remembered at his orphanage, that he would love the country of his birth.

All those prayers were answered. And more, too.

The Spirit of Adoption

Near the end of our journey, we spent several days in Huế, once Vietnam's imperial city. Our visit included a tour of several Buddhist temples located within the red brick walls of the old city. In the quiet space of a temple, I watched as the faithful kneeled before a statue, lost in their own worship. To some, I imagine, this moment would seem fraught with heresy, akin to the idolatry of statue worship that angered the Old Testament God. I imagine, too, that some—including my well-meaning relative—might have advised getting my sons away from the supplicants, lest they be infected by the bad religion being practiced there.

We lingered. My sons, hot and tired and rarely still, walked through the temple quietly, aware of the need for reverence, if not aware of why. For once, they were not poking each other, making jokes, or begging for a treat.

Then, in the corner of the room, I saw him: a boy about Benjamin's age, wearing a simple robe, his hair shaved save for a small curl on his forehead. An acolyte of some kind, he stood beside a monk, assisting him in temple duties. Seeing my son near this young boy, I thought: this could be Benjamin's life, had we not adopted him. Rather than watching Spongebob religiously, trading baseball cards, or grumbling about school, Benjamin could have been here, in a temple, learning the principles of Buddha, studying hours each day under a master, sitting still beside worshipping tourists. And I felt again the sense that has pervaded me since we first adopted my boys. That God, my God, would not have condemned Benjamin to hell had he remained in Vietnam. That he and I needed no prayers of protection from the beautiful traditions of this heritage.

That the mysteries of God would have been open to Benjamin, even if, living in Biên Hòa with his birth family, he had never received the gospel.

On the last day of our trip, we attended a Catholic mass in Hanoi. We were all a little road weary by then, ready for our imminent return to a quiet cul-de-sac, cooler Oregon weather, and a chance to eat home-cooked food. Wanting to experience just a little bit more of Vietnam, but having grown weary of war memorials and history museums, we decided to try church.

The cathedral was nearly empty for its late-morning service, and we found a space near the middle, while white folks and Vietnamese filled in around us, clearly familiar with each other. This was their church community. When the priest began his first litany, we realized that this service would be in French and that only my husband would understand what was happening. My two tired boys, hot and sticky and bored, leaned their bodies close into mine and I held them against me, grateful for this moment of rest. While they dozed, I listened to the priest sharing sacraments with people I did not know, in a tongue I did not understand. In all its familiarity—the crucifix, the twelve stations of the cross, the priest's vestments—this too was a mysterious space to me, God present to me in both the known and the unknown.

So I open myself to this God who lives through the ministry of a Vietnamese priest sharing the bread and cup in a European tongue I don't understand. And to God speaking through a Hindu wedding ceremony, high in the foothills of northern India. And to God, working through the Buddhist acolyte, kneeling to worship in Huế. This is the same God who has extended grace to me, allowing me—in all my imperfections—to raise two imperfectly perfect boys. While I am perplexed most by the mystery of this grace, of this gift, I do not fear it. Instead, I hold God's mystery as close as I do two tired boys sweating beside me in a Hanoi cathedral. For I am always aware that God loves my sons, cherishes them, cares for them.

And would do so, even had we never met.

9

Overcoming

JERE WITHERSPOON

Writing this essay about my adoption story has brought healing. Unfortunately, the experience was needlessly fraught with hurt. As we navigate the crossroads and crucibles in our lives, we have a choice either to embrace a victim mentality or to seize the opportunity to learn from those experiences and somehow become a better person because of them. When we choose the latter, we discover the courage and wisdom it takes to prevent the passing on of heartaches and unhealthy perspectives to those we love the most. Fortunately, my story has a happy ending. Though it is birthed out of pain and disappointment, love and grace are the victors in the end.

My heart still aches for the young woman, just fifteen years of age, who did not receive unconditional love during one of the most difficult times of her life. My heart also aches for my mother, as I now understand that she didn't know how to love me because her mother never taught her how. The power in my story is found in overcoming. The conduit for this is unconditional love.

In August 1973, through a little-known medical phenomenon, I conceived a son without actually having intercourse. At the innocent age of fifteen years, I considered sex to be mating: an action performed by a buck and a ewe to produce the lambs I bred for 4-H. The birds and the bees were explained to me in the context of calves playing leapfrog in the field.

Although I was a typical teenager I was not experienced or savvy in the ways of sex. I attracted the attention of many boys due to my sense of humor, my bubbly personality, and my overdeveloped breasts. Like many of my friends, I spent weekends at parties making out with guys, but never did I consider giving up my viginity, nor was I asked to. I flirted but did so without any unwarranted consequence.

I met the father of my baby one year at church camp. He lived an hour from me so we got to know each other during the weekends when either he came to my house or I took the bus to his. For several months, we enjoyed a nice relationship typical to most high school students. While he was a few years older than me, neither of us seemed experienced in the ways of sexual relationships.

Both of us came from homes that taught the traditional Christian view of sexual behavior: premarital sex is a sin, and you'd better not do it or you're going to hell. Although my parents were educators, they didn't do a good job explaining what was going on in my adolescent body. To be fair, both my mom and dad were just trying to keep their heads above water, and dealing with teenagers was not one of my mom's strengths.

The little I knew about sex was witnessed on our farm. So when my boyfriend and I spent a weekend together at my house—alone—our sexual encounter was awkward, messy, and quite disgusting.

Despite popular belief, you don't need to have intercourse to become pregnant. A man's semen contains millions of wiggly sperm that have one destination in mind. Their whole purpose is to look for a little moisture to use as a conduit to find a woman's vagina and fertilize her egg. Likewise, there are millions of sperm in the pre-ejaculate that is emitted from the penis once it is erect. Obviously, intercourse is the best way to get pregnant, but just having those little sperm swimming around on the moist parts on the outside of one's vagina can produce the same results. Perhaps I impregnated myself when, after the encounter, I went to the bathroom and washed that goo off my inner thighs and vulva. What I know to be true—and this was confirmed by the doctor who delivered my baby—was that I was a virgin when I delivered my firstborn son.

Somehow my parents found out about the secret rendezvous, and my boyfriend and I never connected in a meaningful way again. My parents, I am sure, wanted to protect me from having sex with this guy. Little did they know, the result of their worst fears was already growing inside my fifteen-year-old body.

The Spirit of Adoption

It wasn't until I missed my period for three months in a row that I began to suspect the unimaginable. During my morning classes at school, I experienced the effects of morning sickness, especially when I walked into science class.

Moving from month to month, I continued to live with this secret. My strong abdominal muscles kept the growing baby from exposing itself to the outside world until I was about five months along. The fashion attire of choice at our school was blue jeans and baggy T-shirts, the perfect clothing under which to hide a growing belly.

After four months went by and my period was still missing, at some level I had to acknowledge that my condition was a little more serious than the flu.

I had no one to walk with me through this experience. My youth group leaders at church were more backward and judgmental than my own parents. Though I was raised in the glory years of the sexual revolution, conversations about sexuality did not happen when I was hanging out with my girlfriends. I felt that if someone knew my secret, I wouldn't be accepted any longer. Since I didn't know how my friends were behaving "behind closed doors," I could only perceive their experiences through my own paradigm of shame. Looking back, I wish I had had someone in my life with whom I could have been transparent.

Running away seemed to be the only logical solution. I am sure that I ran through all the people in my life who might have offered refuge. The list was pretty short (something I made sure I paid attention to when I had children of my own). I wrote a long letter to my aunt. She wrote me back, encouraging me to tell my parents. A phone call from her made my mother suspicious, and soon my long-guarded secret was no longer mine alone. The moment I had feared all those months was finally upon me.

My parents did not disappoint me. My mom reacted in the very manner I feared she would. In the eyes of my mom, I had brought unspeakable shame to our family. My mom took it hard, asking me how I could do this to her. My father's response was, "At least we know she's fertile."

Throughout the entire experience, my father, who suffered from rheumatoid arthritis, seemed to take a backseat to my mom and her reaction. This is something he did for most of my life, no matter the situation. While he didn't overreact, he also didn't have the ability to protect me from my mom's wrath and judgment.

My world began to unravel around me. My home, never much of a refuge, was unbearable. My sin and shameful behavior could not be exposed to others. What would our friends and family think? Quiet conversations between my parents excluded my siblings and me. There was a blanket of secrecy in our home. Years later I found out that my siblings had been asked to lie to friends and family about the truth of my condition and keep the "family secret."

I understand now that my parents were responding out of their own worldview and interpretation of Scripture. From their perspective, girls like me were scorned and shunned. In the 1930s and 1940s—my parents' generation—girls who found themselves pregnant and unmarried were sent away by their parents. One Mother's Day when my children were in college, my daughter Kalie gave me a book by Ann Fessler titled *The Girls Who Went Away: The Hidden History of Women who Surrendered Children for Adoption in the Decades Before Roe vs. Wade*. Few of the case studies in this book mirrored my own experience, as most of the women who were featured in this book were from my mom's generation. Reading this book as an adult gave me insight into what my parents were experiencing. However, I still can't wrap my head around how parents can push their child away during a time in her life when she needs her parents' love the most.

My parents did take the advice of Pastor Roy Hicks, and I have always felt that Roy Hicks saved me from utter ruin. Roy was the pastor of Eugene Faith Center. Although we didn't attend at the time, my mom knew people who did, and they likely suggested we go to Roy for counseling. I remember sitting in his office, listening to my mom rattle on about our predicament. As usual, I was embarrassed by my mother's behavior. At the end of my mom's rant, Roy looked over at me with a twinkle in his eye and told us about a woman he knew who managed a home for unwed mothers in downtown Los Angeles. It was a refuge for girls like me who needed to find a place to endure the final months of their pregnancy. This was the perfect solution for all of us.

Early in the month of February, my dad drove me down to L.A. As a parent, I cannot imagine sending my daughter away during the most traumatic time in her life. The journey south seemed pleasant enough, yet I can only imagine what my dad was going through. As we drove, my mind was on what I was missing back home. My ewe would be delivering lambs soon. My brother's pig was going to farrow within weeks. My horse would go unridden for months. I'd be missing out on parties with my friends.

Would I ever see the father of my baby again? What was in store for me in Los Angeles?

Booth Maternity Group Home, run by the Salvation Army in the Lincoln Heights area of Los Angeles, was already on its way to becoming obsolete by 1974. The once-thriving maternity clinic now was a set for Hollywood films or television shows. In the dorm-style rooms of one wing, the girls created a community in response to their common condition. School wasn't far away. In fact, we just had to walk downstairs and past the cafeteria into the basement.

My roommate was a girl my age. Her parents were going to adopt her baby and raise it as their own. It would be her sibling. Even now, I wonder how that worked out for them. Another girl had planned to adopt out her child as well; like me, she wasn't ready to be a mom. One girl had been raped. She was being forced to give up her child. Secretly, she wanted to keep it because she loved babies. The four of us became fast friends.

Living in downtown Los Angeles allowed for some great adventures. Ethnic foods of all kinds were available on every street corner. The entire community was a whole new world for me.

Comfort and love came to me in the body of a beautiful German shepherd puppy I found wandering the streets in our neighborhood. Heidi was probably about four months old. I secretly kept her in the back patio at the home for several weeks before we were found out by one of the house moms. Thankfully, one of the teachers at our school was willing to take her and care for her.

Some weekends I would spend with my aunt's family near Pasadena. My cousin was several months old at the time. Shirley was (and is) a wonderful cook. Between the food in my neighborhood and weekends at Shirley's, it is no wonder I gained fifty pounds in L.A.!

My family also had friends in Colton, California, near Riverside. The Christiansen family had been a part of our family since we lived in San Diego during my early childhood. Andrew was a chiropractor who had been a part of my healing when my back was injured during a horseback ride when I was eleven or twelve. Andrew and Edith invited me out to spend weekends with them. The memories that I have of this elderly couple continue to warm my heart. Their warmth and care for me provided healing for my soul. Edith ended up at the hospital with me during the delivery of my son.

An added bonus was their twenty-one-year-old grandson, Christofer. He and I had met years before when I was "a little squirt." Looking back on my relationship with Chris, I can't help feeling deep sadness. Being a love-starved teenager, I accepted the attention he offered to me. What started out as a friendship quickly swelled into a romance. Over the three months that I spent in Los Angeles, Chris filled the void and gave me a relationship with a man that even the youngest mothers at Booth craved. The sight of his beat-up yellow Chevy van became a source of comfort as we explored all that Los Angeles County had to offer. From BBQs on the beach to art shows in the valley, weekend jaunts to flea markets—Chris opened his heart to me, and I melted into his.

For me the relationship ended when I returned to my home in Oregon. A visit from Chris later that summer solidified the end, as he saw for himself that my heart had moved on. I regret the impulsiveness of my youth and the heartache I must have caused him.

With my weekends busy between my aunt's house and Chris, the time in between was also filled with activities. Besides school, we had counseling sessions. The counselor my group had was a young woman, probably about twenty-eight years old. I had an instant crush on her. Looking back, I now realize she was unlike anyone I had ever met before. She told us that when she and her husband found themselves pregnant, they decided that the timing wasn't right. So they agreed to terminate the pregnancy. This was the first time I had ever had a conversation with someone about what an abortion entailed. Although I didn't fully understand the complexities of this woman's experience, her story did help me in formulating my own opinion on abortion. Having the opportunity to hear an opposing viewpoint would help me accept situations in my children's lives in the future.

Other activities, besides exploring the neighborhood, were brought to us by the fact that Booth Maternity Group Home had a hospital connected to the dormitory. Due to the lack of unwed mothers using the medical facilities, the hospital had been shut down and was now used as a Hollywood movie or TV set. While I was living there, two movies were filmed: *The Healers*, starring John Forsyth, and *The Other Side of the Mountain,* starring Beau Bridges and Marilyn Hassett. One Monday evening I sat in the TV room with John Forsyth watching Monday Night Football. Interestingly enough, the movie *The Healers* was shown on TV the night my son was born. I didn't know this until doing research about my time in Los Angeles.

The Spirit of Adoption

As I reflect on my time there, I fully believe that God intervened and allowed me to get away from the unhealthy environment of my home. While I didn't have any type of relationship with Jesus, God's love and care was evident to me. As hurtful as it was that my parents weren't there for me, other people came into my life to fill the void. I wasn't alone.

As April turned into May, plans were made for my mom to travel to Los Angeles to pick me up. Her time frame for this journey was short, so labor needed to happen at a certain time. Apparently, my baby wasn't cooperating, so I was sent to the doctor so that he could break my water.

Strapped into the stirrups with the nurse at my head, the doctor peered between my legs with a long, stemmed hook. He fiddled around with things down there and then peered up and said, "Well, I see you are still a virgin. Lucky you." At the time I had no idea what he meant.

Labor was horrible. Strapped to a bed with an IV, I remember being very uncomfortable. The experience of this birth would later make me shun hospitals and choose homebirths for my daughters and son. Forceps pried my son from my body, and he was whisked away from the delivery room. Labor had been hard, and while I think I had a spinal block, I was groggy and have little memory of the events after the baby's birth. Due in part to my decision to put my baby up for adoption, I did not have the chance at that moment to see my son.

As I lay in my hospital bed in a private room (away from the mothers with babies), my only visitors were the nurses and my mom, who dropped by to say we would be driving home the next day. It is hard for me to imagine not receiving any comfort from my mom, but I have no memory of such an effort on her part.

Later that night one of the nurses came into my room. She was carrying a baby. My baby. As she entered the room she said, "Every mother needs to see their baby. I know you have a no-contact order but you need to hold your baby." She carefully dropped this dark-haired baby into my arms. As she left the room, she glanced over her shoulder and said, "I'll be back in fifteen minutes."

I peeled the blanket away from his face and stared. He looked just like his father, for my family was all born blond. This child resembled another family. Little mews came from his lips as he settled into my awkward embrace. I don't remember crying, but I remember telling him that he would be better off with a mom and a dad. I reminded him that I was just sixteen years old.

As the fifteen minutes stretched into what seemed like forever, the nurse returned with a bottle. She checked him out, making sure he was okay, and then showed me how to place the nipple into his mouth. He latched onto that nipple and began to suck. It was nothing like the ferocity of the lambs I was used to feeding. I couldn't take my eyes off of him, little Christofer Jo. I named him for the man who helped me through the final months of my pregnancy, and my girlfriend back home, on whose birthday he was born.

The nurse returned just as he was finishing his tiny little bottle. As she reached down to take my son, she gave me a look that was both loving and sorrowful at the same time. His new family was coming to take him in the morning, and I would likely never see him again. This sweet lady knew what I could not imagine. I said goodbye, and she quietly left the room. And that was it. That was the end of chapter one of my adoption story. Little did I know that this experience would shadow me for the rest of my life.

Returning to Oregon towards the end of the school year proved to be the best thing for me. Elections for student government positions were taking place in June. I decided to run for office and won the role of vice president of my junior class. No one said a word (to my face) about my weight gain. My future husband, with whom I went to high school, says that everyone at first wondered where I had gone. Then, when I returned, they all wondered why I had gained so much weight. Life went on as usual for me, as I got back into my group of friends who welcomed me with open arms. Fearing that I would lose them if I told them the truth, I listened to my mom's advice and kept silent, at least for a time. Eventually I found that it was not a big deal that I had a baby. In fact, one of my friends told me after we graduated that she had three abortions in high school. We were all doing the same thing, just experiencing different results.

I started dating Wade at the end of my junior year in high school. We married at the crazy age of twenty in 1978.

After being married for three years, my husband and I decided to start a family. This proved to be more difficult than the first time I got pregnant. In fact, by the third year of trying I began to believe that God was punishing me for having a baby in high school. Thankfully, my friend Denise helped me understand that God does not work that way. Another year would go by before I got pregnant with Brenna. Through her life, healing began to take place in my mind and heart—healing not from the wounds of having a baby in high school, but the damage that was done from my mother's harsh reaction and lack of compassion. Early on, I determined I would make every effort not to repeat my mother's behavior.

Nineteen months after Brenna was born, we welcomed Kalie into the world. Mothers often wonder how they could possibly love another child as much as they love their first. For me, the love poured out naturally. Each of my daughters was different. I loved each of them beyond words. In 1990, while living and working in Papua New Guinea with missionary kids, we had a surprise in the form of our third child, a son. Jesse would forever be the balm of Gilead for my soul.

With each passing year, a strong urge developed in my heart and mind. I began to tell my children over and over again that nothing they could ever do would make me stop loving them. Books like *Love You Forever* by Robert Munsch and Sheila McGraw filled our bookshelves. As the children got older, other influences would cause Wade and me to be more direct as we taught our children.

When the girls were in third and fourth grade, there was a teenager at their school who was pregnant. This seventeen-year-old had returned from Asia with her family, and they settled into the small Christian school our family attended.

As I had when we lived in Papua New Guinea, I reached out to teenagers who found themselves pregnant. So I connected with this young woman, and I often took her to coffee during the last part of the school day. One day I dropped her off at the same time and place where I was to pick up the girls from school. Kalie saw me talking to this young lady. When Kalie got in the car, she looked at me and said, "What were you doing talking to *her*? Don't you know she's pregnant and not married?"

I knew right then that Wade and I needed to have a conversation with the girls about my experiences in an effort to show them the value of God's grace. Wade and I went to great lengths to extend acceptance and love to all teenagers, but especially those who journeyed down a more difficult path in life, and we wanted our children to do the same.

That next Christmas break we found ourselves driving to southern California. This long journey afforded us the perfect opportunity to share my past with the girls. Both Wade and I agreed that he would be the one to tell them the story. So after one pit stop, we positioned Jesse up front (he was too young at this time to understand) while Wade sat in the back of the van with Brenna and Kalie. With great finesse, Wade painted a lovely picture of my story. Each of them had a completely different reaction. Brenna refused to believe it, and Kalie responded, "How could you marry Mom after she did such a horrible thing?"

Although I was driving, my ears were fully tuned to the conversation taking place in the back of the van. I glanced down at Jesse, who was listening to *Veggie Tales*. While the reactions of my daughters were vastly different, I knew that their young hearts had just taken in a lot of information. There was more work to be done in helping them understand grace.

After that conversation with the girls, I felt compelled to go through crisis pregnancy counseling. I felt my experiences could help young women who were dealing with an unplanned pregnancy. The daylong training took place minutes from my house. As the morning approached the midway point, the director closed the morning session with several stories about the young women who came to them from homes where they had no support. With each story I felt a surge of emotion within me. I began to panic, as I feared that I would burst into deep, uncontrollable crying as the speaker concluded. I barely got out of there before what I feared came to pass. As I drove home, the sobbing escalated.

My entrance into our house interrupted the easy Saturday morning of our household. Wade was at the table reading the paper and drinking coffee. The smell of pancakes still lingered in the air. The kids were engrossed in eating their breakfasts and watching cartoons. My entrance captured their attention, and through the sobbing I managed to utter something like, "If you girls or any of your friends ever find yourselves pregnant, or in trouble with anything, you can always come to me. I will always be there for you."

Years later Brenna would tell me that at the time her mind was unable to understand what I meant during my emotional explosion. But as she grew older she saw the effects on her friends when their parents didn't stand with them. Brenna says she always knew that she wouldn't have to experience the confusion, judgment, and rejection that she saw her friends experience.

Kalie was always such a tender, sweet child. Her compassion was evident in so many ways. Perhaps that is why I was surprised by her reaction to learning that I had a baby when I was in high school. Thankfully, as Kalie got older she gained more understanding, wisdom, and grace. The whole experience turned into a powerful teaching tool for all of us.

Letting our children know the truth was important to my husband and me. We all hope that someday our son and brother will find us. In time, over a dinner of sushi, I shared my story with Jesse.

The Spirit of Adoption

Driving many of my decisions about communicating with my children, especially the girls, about love, sex, and relationships was the reality of what was missing from my life when I was their age. I was committed to reversing the behavioral attitudes that my mother had taught me.

My best efforts to create an environment where my daughters felt comfortable discussing with me their personal experiences with the opposite sex were often met by my own self-doubt. Yet in their own ways, both Brenna and Kalie have shown me how my efforts to change the direction of my harmful upbringing allowed us to share more intimately than I have ever dreamed about sharing with my own mother.

When I first heard the song "You Cannot Lose My Love" by Sara Groves, I was reduced to tears. This song became my theme, and ultimately I made photo books for each of my children with the lyrics to this song printed beneath a variety of photos from their childhood.

> Many things can be misplaced;
> Your very memories be erased.
> No matter what the time or space,
> You cannot lose my love.
> You cannot lose,
> You cannot lose,
> You cannot lose my love.

Over the years I would have many opportunities to practice loving unconditionally. I know I failed many times and have made many mistakes, but in the depth of my soul I have only wanted to love my children unconditionally.

After Brenna graduated from college, an incident happened that helped me see that indeed my heart lived on the side of unconditional love and grace.

Arriving home one afternoon, I walked across the street to the mailbox. As I crossed back toward the house, I noticed a small piece of paper along the driveway. I picked it up and saw that it was a credit card receipt. As I walked over to the nearby garbage can, I scanned the words on the receipt and threw it away. Taking several steps away from the garbage, it finally struck me what the words on the receipt meant. The receipt was from Planned Parenthood, from Brenna's account, for the amount of $500.

My knees weakened, and I lost my breath. The first thought that came to my mind was that Brenna had had an abortion and she went through the whole thing alone, without me by her side. My heart was breaking.

Two days went by before I had a chance to talk with her. After I recounted the story of finding the receipt, she reminded me about the situation her friend was in. After an ugly divorce, her friend, a single mother, had a one-night stand that ended in an unwanted pregnancy. Brenna loaned her the money for the medical procedure. I was proud of her for setting her own ideals aside and loving her friend in this way. She kept the door open for further conversation because she didn't judge her friend's actions, but rather said, "What can I do to help?"

Kalie has honored me in the way she trusted me regarding her own sexuality as she developed her relationship with her boyfriend, now her husband. It was an honor to have her trust me and to see how mature she was in making decisions about her own life.

As a woman with grown children, with my first grandchild on the way, the emotions of the deepest wounds from my pregnancy in high school still erupt. A friend recently asked me to share my "survivor story" for her nonprofit group called Survivor's Truths. This organization creates media projects that support the recovery of groups affected by violence or discrimination. As I reflected upon my friend's request I had a hard time putting any of my life stories up against the stories I know from this organization. Compared to the stories of those helped by this nonprofit organization, my story did not seem to be of any value.

When I spoke to my husband about my dilemma, he helped me see that I had a great survivor story to tell. He helped me see that because of my experience in high school, I had made decisions to love my children unconditionally, that indeed I had a story worth sharing.

I planned my story on paper and then carefully recorded it on my computer. After several attempts to get through the story without crying, I realized I was unable to do so. The statement that keeps haunting me is, "How can a mother abandon her daughter at the time in her life when she needed her the most?"

And yet, in the midst of that abandonment I was able to discover a better path to follow for my own life and, ultimately, a better way for my family: unconditional love, acceptance, and commitment, being there for each other no matter what.

Over the years, and even when we dated in high school, Wade has been incredibly supportive and understanding. His desire to help our daughters understand my story and his time spent listening to me when I was burdened with the emotions from the abandonment I felt as a young girl have been a source of comfort and strength for me. And now, when the father of the baby recently contacted me after thirty-five years to get information for his quest to find his son, Wade gave me wisdom and insight that only a loving and gracious husband can give.

Finding my son was not something I felt I had the right to pursue. However, I have done whatever I can to make it easy for him to find me. Online adoption websites have made it easy for anyone to create an account so one can search for birth parents, sons or daughters. A few years ago I launched a search on a new website. I received emails from people who gave me really good information about putting a "consent to contact" form in my son's adoption file with the adoption agency. That was something I could easily accomplish. I was hoping that my son would have placed a similar form in his file for me to find. I was disappointed that this was not the case.

While as a teenager I couldn't imagine keeping my son, the love that I have for him has endured over the last thirty-nine years. Handing my baby to a family that was complete and ready to love him was the best decision for both of us. Adoption doesn't have to mean loss. In my mind I was sharing and giving a gift of incomparable value. I am forever grateful to that nurse who secretly brought my son to me so I could have an intimate moment with him.

I got a tattoo to celebrate my thirtieth wedding anniversary; part of the design included three flowers to represent my three children. After having the tattoo for several months, I began having dreams about the son of my youth. For several nights I had dreams about him at different ages, involved in my life in different ways. One morning I woke up and realized that I didn't have a tattoo to represent his part in my life. I phoned my tattoo artist and made an appointment for the following day. Now I have a flower tattooed on the inside of my wrist on my other arm. Separate from the other flowers, different in color, but still a part of me forever.

There is no doubt in my mind that I would not be the person I am today without the experiences in my life, both the good and the bad. Facing the dark times and allowing positive changes to influence my life have allowed me to create a healthier environment for my children. This fact alone makes me very thankful for all the experiences in my past.

By definition the word *crucible* infers that under certain situations, forces converge to cause change or influence development. I am thankful that through my experiences—my crucibles—I discovered the courage and wisdom needed to not only change the trajectory of my life but the precious lives of my children, and ultimately my grandchildren. With my husband at my side and the Holy Spirit in my heart, my story ends with victory.

10

Where in the Bible Am I?

Kimberly Claassen Felton

I entered adoption reluctantly. Heartbroken from a miscarriage and subsequent years of infertility, I wanted to parent; but I also wanted desperately to feel a baby growing inside me. Marriage, and then pregnancy, had awakened in me a desire to be part of the miracle of birth. I wanted a baby created from *us*. I wanted a little girl with Rob's red curls.

It isn't that I didn't want to adopt, or never felt excited about it. I did. And that excitement was reassuring. I imagined what our adopted girl or boy might look like, but the possibilities were so endless it was overwhelming. Including another family, our child's birth family, in holidays and weekends the rest of our lives was also daunting. But this is what proponents of open adoption encourage, if the birth family desires that involvement. I completed adoption training at our agency feeling like the child never could be simply *our* child.

As someone afraid of making mistakes, I feared creating my own catastrophe. Clear instruction is reassuring. Advice from friends to "just adopt" doesn't count, by the way—particularly when they could plan their families the traditional way with nary a hesitation in procreating. They did not know the heartache or the uncertainty. I would have loved a clear, direct word from God about adoption. None came.

What did come during our five years of fertility exploration was countless blood and urine samples, as well as Rob's own contributions; spreading my legs for prodding and probing, breathing deeply to "just relax" while a disgruntled doctor stuck various instruments into my smallness; cringing or gasping in pain and squeezing Rob's hand until he gasped; two surgeries and a procedure that should never cause so much pain without delivering a baby at the end.

Throughout those years, Rob and I played leapfrog for who was ready to explore adoption. One balmy summer evening, as we walked and talked, he said he was happy to adopt. Sometime; maybe not yet. I wasn't so sure that night. Yet I was the first to stop stalling and begin researching adoption options. But before Rob caught up, I'd lagged behind again in the hope of another doctor, another possibility for bearing a child.

As the story goes for so many would-be parents, we reached the end of what we were willing to try. *I* was at the end—my faith, hope, and love bucket pockmarked with dents and holes. That was when we decided to adopt.

Turning from one journey absent of miracles, we stared into another full of questions. The choice to adopt domestically was easy; we wanted an infant. The answers to other questions were not immediate: How long until a birth mom chooses us? Is she healthy? Will the baby be healthy? How do we justify declining any baby? Will our families accept our child? Will the birth mom change her mind? We discovered adoption is as uncertain and miraculous as pregnancy, and infinitely more intrusive. The adoption agency had their own questions.

While most couples decide to create a family in the privacy of their own bedrooms, we would need approval from the adoption agency to be parents. They requested our tax information, inspected our home, received character references from our friends and family, and interrogated (interviewed) Rob and me together and separately. Our agency was excellent and respectful. Yet I was baffled when the single, twenty-five-year-old caseworker asked us, "Have you healed from your journey of infertility?"

"Do you ever?" I asked her.

I don't know what our journey would have looked like without faith. Faith is an intricate, inseparable part of me. I clung to God; I turned from God. I kicked God out of the room . . . and months later, thanked God for never leaving the house. I sought God through quiet, through weeping, in nature, and in friends. I sought God in the Bible. And I looked for myself in the Bible, for clues about where this journey might lead, what it might mean.

The Spirit of Adoption

Every barren woman mentioned in the Bible was given a child—through pregnancy. Sarah gave birth to Isaac. Rebekah gave birth to Esau and Jacob. Rachel bore Joseph, and later Benjamin. Monah's wife bore Samson. The prophet Samuel was born to Hannah. The Shunammite woman bore a son. Elizabeth gave birth to John the Baptist. The one exception is Michal, daughter of King Saul and wife of King David: childlessness was her punishment.[1]

The Bible narrates the end of Rachel's barrenness with these words: "Then God remembered Rachel, and God listened to her and opened her womb. And she conceived and bore a son, and said, 'God has taken away my reproach.'" *Reproach. God listened. God remembered.* As months on the calendar turned, and each January we replaced the old calendar with a new one, I staggered beneath the reproach of infertility and struggled to understand why God didn't remember me.

I'd like to say I trusted God implicitly, that I eagerly looked for the open windows instead of pushing against the door that wouldn't budge. The best I can claim, though, is that I trust God more now than I did before, that I'm more determined to trust, because I believe the promises are true—promises that declare God's love for me, the good plans established for me, the goodness and justice and rightness of God's very nature and being. I am determined to trust because I know God has never left me.

In my search for encouragement on the new path toward adoption, I turned my eyes from barren-to-pregnant women to examples of adoptive parents in the Bible. It wasn't good news. Sarah spurned her adopted child, Ishmael, and his birth mom, Hagar, with such severity that they escaped into the desert and expected to die. Using the same method of adoption as Sarah, Rachel ordered her maid to share a bed with Jacob, Rachel's husband, and gained two sons through her servant. But it was the sons physically born of Rachel (after God opened her womb) who were greatly favored by their father Jacob—to the detriment of all other siblings.

These stories ended in jealous catastrophes and punched my fear buttons. Would I love my adopted child less than a biological child? Would I be so self-centered as to toss aside a child if I ever gave birth? Adopted children in the Bible did pretty well: Moses led the nation Israel out of Egypt; Esther married the king and helped circumvent a plot to annihilate all Jews;

---

1. References in order of women mentioned: Gen 21, 25, 30; Judg 13; 1 Sam 1; 2 Kgs 4; Luke 1; and 2 Sam 6.

and Jesus (yes, even He was adopted—by Mary's husband, Joseph) did no less than open the way for us to be with God.

I felt pretty good about our adopted child's future; she has great role models. But I was discouraged for myself. Yes, I could look to any number of excellent examples of adoptive parents and families in my community. What I longed for, though, was encouragement through the book God put together for us. The book that says, "Do not fear" and "Be strong and courageous." I wanted to know I could apply those verses to our situation. I needed to know that, somewhere in the Bible, God had included a role model for me in this unexpected journey.

When Rob and I decided to have children, we did not think about asking God if this was the best plan. Of course it was. When we lost our first child and then failed to get pregnant again, that was when the praying began. As we waded further into fertility treatments and the methods of getting pregnant felt less and less natural, my prayers slowly shifted, from "Please let this work!" to "Is this OK? Is this what You want? Could this *please* be what You want?"

As we signed the agreement with an adoption agency and knew birth moms were looking at our photo album, I told Rob I didn't know what to pray. Awkward as fertility treatments were, this was worse: a woman had to give up her child so I could be a mother; we had to determine what skin colors we would graft into our family tree, and what histories of mental illnesses or birth family issues we would accept.

Adoption happens when unhappy circumstances surround a pregnancy, and a woman will not or cannot raise her child. I wanted to ask God for a child, but I could not pray for bad things to happen to another woman.

"How do we pray?" I asked Rob.

"I'm asking God for a child who will thrive in our home," he said.

I could do that. I could trust God to provide exactly what we *all* need. We wanted to be as perfect for this child as it would be for us. We wanted what was best for everyone, including the birth mom.

Four months after signing papers with the agency, a local Hispanic woman chose us for her unborn baby. Eight weeks later, we held our daughter Madeleine in our arms. I fully expected to tumble into love. Instead, I tumbled into unexpected emotional turbulence. As Rob cuddled our daughter for hours on end, marveling at our tiny miracle, I felt the failure of not making him a father myself. I was a fake mom, and guilt washed over me again and again as I remembered the birth mom's tears when she kissed her—our—baby. I still did not have a place to burrow in the Bible, a role model, a story where I could find myself.

In the first couple months after Madeleine's arrival, I was drawn to the book of Esther. Reading once was not enough. I read it a second time, and a third. A fourth. I've always liked Queen Esther's story: she's a young girl, a nobody, so beautiful that she catches the king's eye. She's an orphan, adopted by an older cousin when her parents died. Though I like the story, I cannot explain my compulsion to read and reread it outside of the Holy Spirit—because when I finally saw *it*, I knew God was in the discovery.

"It" was the older cousin, Mordecai, the one who adopted Esther. When Esther was taken to the palace, Mordecai followed and kept an eye on her from a distance. Even when the king made Esther queen, she still respected Mordecai enough to take his advice and do what he said—at risk to her own life. Mordecai acted with such wisdom and discernment that before the book ends, he's second in command of the kingdom. This is what I desperately needed: an adopted parent in the Bible who was loving, fully committed to his adopted child, wise, respected. In the end, Mordecai was a world-changer—first through Esther, and then acting on his own.

Here I found hope, some footsteps to follow. I pray I'll act in such a way that earns Madeleine's respect, and have the discernment to give her good council as she faces life's choices. I pray for eyes to see the gifts and skills given to her, and for determination to delight not in what makes her "like me" but what makes her uniquely her. I pray for a bond between us that comes from God, not from genetics.

When the biblical Rachel finally conceived, she said, "God has taken away my reproach." Adoption has not fully removed my reproach. Pregnancy, for me, remains an unanswered prayer. Though having a daughter removes the sting, twinges of sadness and questions remain. I am content—deeply so—when I see Madeleine's little brown hand nestled in my larger white one. I am her mama. She *is* my daughter. Some people say Madeleine is God's answer to our prayers. I would say God's answer to my prayers for pregnancy was, simply, "No." Madeleine is the "and" part of that answer. "No, you will not get pregnant. *And*, here's an entirely different gift." Adoption does not make up for infertility, nor should it.

It takes faith to let my pain over infertility stand on its own, my prayers echoing back to me, while trusting in the goodness of God and stepping into and embracing an entirely different path. Rather than glossing over the tender ache of what I lost, I will let my loss increase my compassion, wisdom, and discernment as I raise a daughter given to me through another woman's pain. Before Madeleine was ever born, she lost her birth family. As soon as she was born, she gained a new family. Adoption is about loss. And it's about the gifts of sacrifice and love that cannot come without that loss.

Madeleine does not replace the child I lost, or the children I could not have. She is her own person on her own journey. And by faith, I'll walk that journey with her.

11

The *Whole* Story

Revisiting the Unspoken Complexities of Adoption

JACQUELINE N. GUSTAFSON

Sitting in the window seat on our Ethiopian Airlines flight, I watched the sun rise over the Sahara, red and orange tones reflecting off the desert landscape in the early morning hours. Now well over twenty hours into our flight, I knew that we were close. Soon we would be on the ground at the Addis Ababa International Airport. Like many adoptive families, we found ourselves on the journey of a lifetime—traveling more than eight thousand miles from Seattle to Ethiopia to pick up our six-month-old son. We had spent the better part of the previous year doing paperwork, planning, waiting, and then planning and waiting some more. Most adoptive families know this routine well. Although both my husband and I had traveled overseas before and had seen the harsh realities of the developing world, we both knew that Ethiopia would be something entirely different. I knew I would encounter extreme poverty on a scale I had not seen. I also expected that I would be faced with the reality of HIV/AIDS, which is ravaging a nation already devastated by years of famine and war. These aspects of what we were about to encounter were difficult, but I remember smiling as I reflected upon the joy of being united with my son.

The landscape below slowly changed, and we began to see clusters of trees and then small villages. From my vantage point, the Ethiopian countryside looked beautiful, almost reminiscent of the bountiful agricultural valleys of central California. Descending lower, this idyllic scene began to change. Although not without beauty, it became apparent that the landscape below was indeed very far from the idyllic countryside of Napa or Carmel. Even from my seat in the airplane I caught glimpses of hills and valleys ravaged by drought and deforestation. As we drew closer to the city, I could see the sprawling clusters of hovels that were likely home to those who had once made a way of life outside of the city until they were forced to migrate in search of food and work. These images, while transfixing, were only a foreshadowing of what was to come. Somehow I knew, even then, that life would really never be the same for me. What I did not know was that the very essence of my faith would be transformed as well.

Fast forward one month and, naturally, life was different for my family after arriving home from Ethiopia with our son. For one, I was experiencing the trials and joys of being a first-time parent. My husband, Dave, and I had been married for nearly ten years, and although life had dealt us a few difficult blows, some might say we had been living the American Dream. Both Dave and I have been blessed with good educations, upwardly mobile jobs, and the comforts and securities of middle-class life in the United States. Don't get me wrong—this was never our goal. For years both of us had fostered a strong desire to help others, to serve, and to invest not in material things but in things of eternal value. In fact, it was that desire that landed us on the path to adoption in the first place.

Diapers and bottles had replaced spontaneous dinner dates and movies, and the trips to the market seemed to consume the same amount of planning and packing as our previous weekends away. Yet, in the midst of juggling my various roles as wife, mother, and professional, I sensed a subtle transformation of my mind and my spirit. In the quiet moments of solitude during late-night feedings, I found my mind wandering to places and issues that had previously been far from my life. In the hurried activities of the day I sensed this same subtle shift. I knew that becoming a parent could change things; I was learning that becoming an adoptive parent could transform the very essence of my being.

One month earlier, I had looked down from my seat in the airplane, overcome with the sense that life would never be the same. Only over time did I realize that through becoming an adoptive parent I had created an intimate, eternal connection to my son's adoption story. Although I was tempted to allow myself to believe that his story began the day I first held him in my arms, I know this was not true and to live this lie would not honor him or his story. Instead, I decided that I would work to acknowledge his *whole* story, a story that began long before I even so much as heard the sound of his sweet name.

Our Story Is Not the Whole Story

Poverty and social injustice had not been a part of my life story before adopting my son. However, these complex and intertwined elements were a part of my son's story—his story before he became part of our family. I had to acknowledge that he lived before he lived with me, he suffered before he suffered in my arms, and he cried tears of grief and separation before I was there to wipe his tears away. He was someone's child before he was my child. With a full tummy and a warm bed, he lay peacefully sleeping in his room as I watched; the scene was idyllic but hid the harsh realities of his life. A tough start was part of his *whole* story and now, through the spirit of adoption, had forever become a part of my life.

These intertwined elements—poverty, disease, and social injustice—are part of the story for many orphans today and are certainly part of the orphan crisis on a systemic level. "Orphan crisis" is a term that has come to describe the innumerable children, globally, who have lost one or both parents, although the term seems lacking in both clarity of definition and agreement in numbers. According to All God's Children International, a Christian adoption and orphan care organization based in Portland, Oregon, today there are 153 million orphans worldwide, a number that represents close to half of the U.S. population.[1] In addition, it is reported that a mere fraction of a percent, one-tenth of 1 percent, will be adopted.[2] As an adoptive mother, the term "orphan crisis" has a very real, personal significance. In my own home, the orphan crisis represents the many factors that contributed to my own son becoming classified as an orphan. However, my son, once an orphan, is considered "lucky"—representing part of the fraction of 1 percent of orphans to be adopted, that same percent that we often focus on exclusively in the adoption community. This is an important fraction of 1 percent and represents a magnitude of compassion, grace, and

1. All God's Children, "Global Orphan Crisis," para. 1.
2. Ibid.

love from God and from forever families. However, as adoptive families and as advocates of adoption, we must not forget that the orphan crisis also includes the other 99-plus percent of orphaned children who will, for a myriad of reasons, never be adopted.

My son's story, now a part of my own story, is inextricably tied to the orphan crisis. Was it possible that through the *least of these* (Matt 25:40, 45) I had seen the heart of the Father? Had I seen God's heart for the poor, the orphan and the widow, the oppressed? Becoming an adoptive parent who seeks to acknowledge my son's *whole* story has shaken and transformed my faith. I have seen the Father's love for His most forgotten children. That changes everything. The words of Bob Pierce, founder of World Vision, resonate deeply: "Let my heart be broken with the things that break the heart of God." I have no doubt that this is not the only way to encounter such a faith transformation. However, this is my story—my story of how God's redemptive justice was evidenced in the reordering of my heart,[3] how I was transformed by, or through, the spirit of adoption.

Living Out the Whole Story

Two years ago I sat watching TV with my son, preoccupied as I contemplated how much screen time would be too much screen time for his then four-year-old brain (ironically, inherent in the content of this very preoccupation is privilege, wealth, and access that is inconceivable to most of the world). Only fifteen minutes into the program, my son nudged me; pointing to the TV and furrowing his brow, he asked me why those kids on TV didn't have any food—and then he said, "They look like me." As I looked up at the TV I saw that the program had gone to a commercial break; an advertisement for a child relief agency was playing.

No words can express the way in which this and other encounters shake my core and cause me to look straight into the face of injustice and ask what it has to do with my life, what it has to do with my faith. I believe that caring for the orphan and the widow, or working to alleviate poverty and to free the oppressed, have everything to do with God (Jas 1:27). Yet,

---

3. Groody describes social justice as a combination of internal and external justice. The internal serves to restore one's relationship with God, whereas the external restores one's relationship with others. As such, Groody provides a definition for social justice that moves away from reordering the economy, or even social structures, and focuses directly on the reordering of hearts. Groody, *Globalization, Spirituality, and Justice*, 26–27.

I know how very easy it is, especially in the midst of privilege, access, and wealth, to shy away from the work to which our faith calls us. As an adoptive mother, I have come to realize that ignoring this call to action would mean not only failing to experience the fullness of my relationship with God but also dismissing and dishonoring my son's whole story.

My son has now been in our family for over five years. Each day I wrestle with the tension—the tension of the whole story. Even now I do not have all of the answers or know how I might continue to be transformed. I can say that the rest of the world will never look far away again. For me, now, the world is only as far away as my son is from me at any given moment. While I know that my son's story has changed my story and transformed my faith, I am still on a journey to learn what this looks like in action. The Christian community often talks about a personal relationship with our God or with our Savior, Jesus Christ. As a Christian, I do not dismiss the value or purpose of a personal relationship with our Creator, our Savior. In fact, I believe that is the most important relationship a person can have. However, I wonder how that personal relationship is defined if not through active responses to one's community. My experience as an adoptive mother, seeking to acknowledge my son's whole story, has set me on a faith journey to explore this very question.

Transformed Faith in Action

Although many aspects of the orphan crisis deserve exploration, my family has focused on poverty, health care, educational disparities, and human rights. Certainly my coverage of these topics is not intended to be comprehensive, but rather an introductory survey of four issues of paramount importance in understanding the *whole* story for our family. My son's early life, before becoming part of our family, was affected by poverty, health care and educational disparities, and social injustices. If I pretended that his life began when he joined our family, then these elements (poverty, health care, education, and social justice) would not be personal. Yet, my son's life indeed began, and had both meaning and value, long before he joined our family—so, for our family it is personal. As his mother I am his advocate, his champion. Would a mother of a child suffering from another adversity (e.g., childhood cancer, autism, or even bullying) not do the same? The organizations that I mention below are not the only organizations doing excellent work to combat global poverty, bolster health care and education, and protect human rights. Instead, I have included a few organizations that I respect or that have been significant in my family's journey as we work to embrace the whole story and live as active agents of change in what we have now come to embrace as *our* story.

Poverty

One aspect of our story that I've had to embrace is that poverty, in developing nations, is intricately connected to the orphan crisis. The realities of extreme poverty are not only harsh but also far-reaching, with implications not only for economic wellbeing but also maternal and infant health, education, safety, and even human rights. Yet, poverty is one of the most controversial issues, spanning time and culture, in the Christian community. On the one hand, many in the Christian community are inspired by the lives of those such as St. Francis of Assisi, a priest who, while not born into poverty, was so moved by the experience of the poor that he vowed a life of poverty. On the other hand, countless Christians believe that one's wealth is a tangible connection to the blessings and provision of God. Ultimately, I believe God is much more concerned with the condition of our hearts than the state of our material worth (rich or poor). Rich and poor alike act out of selfish greed and ambition, oppose the work of God, and fail to see God's heart for His children. While questions of faith and poverty are certainly worthy of debate, and are part of a much-needed dialogue in our contemporary society, their very essence connotes a certain level of wealth and security that is unknown to much of the world. The existential dilemma created by such questions—to strive for wealth or to embrace poverty in solidarity with the poor—is far from the minds of those living in extreme poverty. For those living in extreme poverty, those struggling to survive in my son's birth country, the questions are very simple. Where will my next meal come from? Which child will I feed? Will we live another day? Do I want to live another day? Questions such as these, asked by birth parents, family members, and the community, characterized and shaped my son's first months of life. These questions are as near to God's heart as the questions that we ask from places of privilege in our lecture halls and our pulpits, or at our plentiful dinner tables.

On the one hand, my lived experience is one of privilege—an existence characterized by just enough wealth and privilege that I can join the debate over the relationship between faith and poverty. On the other hand, my adoptive son's *whole* story is characterized by much simpler questions. An infant or small child, cognitively unable to ask these questions, still experiences the visceral sensation of hunger, lack of security, and an unknown future. As an adoptive mother, I contemplate poverty and its relationship to my son's story; furthermore, I consider my role in alleviating extreme poverty, extreme poverty that undoubtedly contributes to the orphan crisis.

Why do children become orphaned? One can put forward any number of answers. Certainly some children do become orphaned as a direct result of poverty (e.g., loss of one or both parents from malnutrition). Furthermore, poverty is inarguably tied to health, education, and other social justice issues—each one of which results in children being orphaned, together creating an orphan crisis. However, many countless children are considered orphaned and placed for adoption because they do not have a mother or father with adequate resources to care for him or her. In many cases, combating poverty works to support family and cultural preservation and to prevent children from becoming orphaned or in need of an adoptive family.

As an adoptive mother and a strong proponent of adoption, I am sometimes surprised by the anti-adoption theme that can characterize my inner dialogues. I believe that God has called my family to adopt, and we have acted upon this call. Furthermore, I believe that there is strong support for the care of the orphan, and for adoption, in the Scriptures. Yet, I believe that it is because I love my son and because of God's heart for the orphan that I desire to work harder against the causes of the orphan crisis than for adoption. Please don't misunderstand; I believe that adoption is a wonderful opportunity, one made possible by the grace of our loving God. Furthermore, there will always be innumerable situations in which, as a result of tragedy or adversity, adoption is the only option or is the most loving, courageous choice made by a biological parent. Most significantly, the act of adopting a child into the love, relationship, and provision of a forever family is the most beautiful metaphor of my own adoption into God's family. There will always be a need for adoption, and I will always support adoption. Yet, some organizations work against adoption, believing that preventing the orphaning of children and working for family and cultural preservation must take precedence. Other organizations work ardently to bring together adoptive parents with children in need while failing to address the root causes of the children's needs. I don't presume to understand all of the intricacies that inform the motives of even the best of these organizations; however, I have come to embrace the philosophy that orphans today need families, while orphans tomorrow need not be orphans. In other words, I do not believe that we can ever turn our back on even one child in need of a forever family for the sake of focusing on the big picture. At the same time, we must not forget the big picture—we must work to address root causes that result in children becoming orphaned and needing adoptive families in the first place.

Poverty, and its relationship to other root causes of the orphan crisis, becomes a central focus for me, and I must give poverty alleviation significant attention. As with any cause, we can begin in our own homes and our own communities—working to instill in our children the value of their many blessings as well as a heart of service for the less fortunate. For example, in my own home we have dedicated Wednesday nights as "rice and beans" night; each Wednesday, for dinner, we consume a simple meal of rice and beans. Our goal is twofold. First, consuming a meal of rice and beans is very inexpensive, and by engaging in this practice once a week, we are able to increase slightly the margins in our budget that can be used for other expenditures (charitable donations and investments and/or increasing our ability to purchase sustainable and fair trade grocery items). The second goal, initially an afterthought that has since superseded the first, is to engage in regular activities in solidarity with those in extreme poverty—those subsisting on regular diets of little more than rice and beans. Wednesday night's "rice and beans" regularly brings me to a place of reflection, gratitude, and humility. In addition to simple acts and small sacrifices, significant work must also be done for the poor in the way of community and economic development. Numerous nonprofit organizations work to alleviate poverty and to promote sustainable community and economic development both locally and globally. In an effort to reduce global poverty and to combat the orphan crisis, you might consider supporting an organization with a mission consistent with your goals and philosophy. For example, if you want to become involved locally, you might consider volunteering with or financially contributing to an organization like Habitat for Humanity, which provides decent, safe, affordable housing to low-income families.[4] In addition, through numerous social enterprise organizations, you can contribute to the development and sustainability of the global community.

---

4. Habitat for Humanity, "About."

Health Care

General health, and specifically maternal and infant health, like poverty, is indissolubly connected to the orphan crisis. Cognitively I know the correlations. It was at the Center for Adoption Medicine, at a local university, that I experienced this reality. My son, then six months old, received his first well-child check and reliable immunizations. He was evaluated as average in size and in good physical and psychological health—termed a "developmental miracle" by the pediatrician. My son, average by the standards upheld in the developed world, was a "developmental miracle," given his story.

Sickness and disease are not confined to one area or people, but rather affect all people in every community, sparing no geographic region or era in human history.[5] However, health promotion, disease prevention, and medical care and treatment vary greatly throughout the world today. Even in the wealthiest, most developed regions, thousands suffer needlessly as a result of inadequate health care services. In the poorest, most underdeveloped parts of the world, health care systems are, at best, only embryonic. Whether the patient is an elderly American woman unable to afford medication for debilitating arthritis or a young Ethiopian girl with no available treatment for an obstetric fistula, the consequences of global health care disparities are acute, life-altering realties and worthy of considerable attention. As a well-educated American woman, I can reason that maternal and infant health clearly links to the orphan crisis. However, more importantly, as an adoptive mother seeking to understand the *whole* story, I want to understand why children become orphaned as a result of inadequate health care and how I can combat the orphan crisis through health promotion.

Lack of family planning, maternal health, and infant health directly result in mothers who are unable to parent. HIV, malaria, tuberculosis, and other fully preventable diseases rob children of one or both parents and, ultimately, further propagate the orphan crisis. Furthermore, it seems that health care disparities have been unusually cruel to women and children in developing nations. For example, pregnancy- and childbirth-related complications are the leading cause of death among adolescent girls in developing nations.[6] As with many issues, poverty, education, and justice issues further exacerbate the problem through the perpetuation of systems that force girls into sexual relationships before their bodies are physically

---

5. Since the fall as recorded in Gen 3.
6. Murray, *From Outrage to Courage*, 65.

developed and able safely to bear children. In some cases, children become orphaned because of lack of available medical treatment or intervention, and in other cases simply for lack of adequate health promotion. For example, some young women, too young to safely deliver a baby and with no adequate medical assistance available, die in childbirth, often leaving behind a baby with no available caregiver. In other instances, a mother or father contracts HIV and then eventually dies, often leaving behind multiple children who have no hope of survival without the intervention of a family member, friend, or community organization.

In this era of rapid globalization, people have greater access to information and the ability to connect to people on the other side of the world. On the one hand, location has become irrelevant; with the ease of technology one can work, purchase, or sell goods, or even carry on a relationship, with people across the globe. On the other hand, location is entirely relevant—when it comes to health care, location still determines whether you will live or die. As an adoptive mother of a child from a diseased, ravaged nation, I suggest—no, I proclaim—that where you live should not determine if you live. You could argue that we all die at some point. Indeed, death is inescapable, but mothers and fathers die of preventable diseases, curable ailments, and controllable maladies in situations that people in developed countries find unacceptable.[7] In the adoptive community, we must come to embrace work for maternal and infant health as work for the orphan and against one cause of the orphan crisis. Personally, I began to embrace the reality of this challenge even before returning home from Ethiopia with my son. While in Ethiopia, I spent an afternoon at the Hamlin Fistula Hospital in Addis Ababa. Although I have spent time with the sick and have visited hospitals in many regions of the world, my encounter at the Hamlin Fistula Hospital remains the single most poignant example of the consequences of health care disparities for women in the developing world. The hospital, founded by missionary doctors Reginald and Catherine Hamlin, exists to serve the specific needs of women suffering from obstetric fistula injuries in Ethiopia. Obstetric fistulas[8] are a debilitating birth injury resulting from

---

7. Paul Farmer, in his book *Pathologies of Power,* argues that research and advocacy work must be done in order to advance the social and economic rights of the poor precisely because the world's poorest people suffer from grave health inequities.

8. Obstetric fistulas result not only in physical suffering and malfunction but also social isolation and rejection. Assisted births and medical technology have nearly eliminated fistula injuries in most of the world; however, fistulas continue to plague women in developing nations, with an estimated one hundred thousand new cases per year (Hamlin, "What Is a Fistula?").

compounding factors including unassisted deliveries, young maternal age, and malnourishment.[9] Catherine Hamlin is a woman who truly understands the connection between culture, health, and justice and has sacrificed herself to bring healing to the world's poorest and most marginalized. One could say that she is my hero. To learn more about obstetric fistulas, or to support young women in need of restorative surgery, contact Hamlin Fistula International or watch the acclaimed PBS film *A Walk to Beautiful*, which chronicles the journey of several young Ethiopian women affected by obstetric fistulas.

Furthermore, numerous organizations work to provide emergency medical services as well as to build sustainable health care systems in developing regions of the world. I have personally been impressed by the work of Medical Teams International, a Christian global health organization that provides both emergency medical aid as well as holistic development programs. Other organizations have also emerged with the expressed intent of working for health promotion and disease prevention. My own family, inspired by the adoption of our son, has become involved in a WASH (water, sanitation, and hygiene) sector organization called Charity Water. Charity Water operates according to the motto "water changes everything" and works to improve health care and quality of life through improving clean water supply in developing nations.[10]

Education

I am a professor and a university administrator, an educator by profession. I have spent my entire life either receiving education or providing education. There are few things that I value as much as high-quality education and its transformative value. However, as an adoptive mother, I now must examine two separate, yet connected, facets of education. First, how do educational disparities contribute to the orphan crisis? Second, how can education be leveraged as a transformative tool to alleviate the orphan crisis?

Several years ago I found myself sitting in a small family restaurant in a favela in Rio de Janeiro, Brazil. Over a plate of tripe, black beans, and rice, I attempted to carry on a conversation with my colleagues, yet our voices were nearly muted by the roar of the two televisions mounted on the wall—one blasting MTV and the other *Rambo*. Outside the restaurant,

9. Hamlin, "What Is a Fistula?"
10. Charity Water, "Why Water?"

children who should have been in school were playing in the street, too poor to afford the supplies. While I am neither a proponent of globalization nor an opponent, I am perhaps a critic of the direction of globalization. The spreading and melding of cultures and ways of being is likely inevitable, and in some cases, it comes with great reward. However, I experience a great sense of dissatisfaction knowing that MTV and McDonald's have taken root in developing nations, yet even a basic education remains out of reach for many living in poverty, especially for poor girls.

As an adoptive mother, I ask myself how education or the lack of education contributes to the orphan crisis. Certainly there are education disparities between nations. However, perhaps more significant are the educational disparities that exist within nations. Take, for example, a community in a sub-Saharan African nation. This community may be fortunate enough to have basic education available in a one-room schoolhouse. However, in this one-room school house, one will find very few young girls present. This compels us to ask, where are the girls? Why are they not in school with their male counterparts? A variety of explanations has been offered. First, in many places, young girls are still seen as property, some thing, that at the time of marriage will be sold to another community. Therefore, the question of a girl's education quickly becomes nothing more than an economic issue. A father may ask, "Why would I invest in my daughter's education just to send her away? That education will never improve our family or our community." Second, young women make up a huge part of the labor force in developing nations. Again, this becomes an economic question—many communities simply believe that they cannot afford sending girls to school when those girls are needed in the fields and the homes. Finally, health care and hygiene issues contribute to the absence of girls in the classroom. Certainly both sexes miss far too many days of school as a result of illness and disease. Countless days are lost to preventable illness—malaria resulting from lack of mosquito netting or even something as simple as chronic diarrhea from an inadequate clean water supply. However, young girls also miss school as a result of inadequate education and hygiene practices related to menstruation. In many places, a girl is simply required to stay home from school during menstruation. Furthermore, it is reported that school enrollment statistics indicate enrollment but not attendance.[11] In many communities, girls are enrolled in school but do not attend. As such, statistics demonstrate the enrollment for girls is only slightly lower

---

11. Murray, *From Outrage to Courage*, 36.

than enrollment for boys; these numbers likely do not portray an accurate picture of who is and who is not receiving an education.

Are these educational issues for females connected to the orphan crisis? According to both the United Nations and the World Bank, education for girls is regarded as critical to poverty alleviation, health improvement, and community development.[12] A young woman who has not received an education is unable to earn income enough to support herself and her children; dependence upon a male partner or her community is therefore the only chance of survival for her and her children. However, both health care and justice issues make this relationship tenuous at best. In some cases, support from a male partner is lost as a result of illnesses such as HIV. In other cases, women, especially those who become physically ill (e.g., who suffer from an obstetric fistula or are injured or disabled), are abandoned, left to care for themselves and their children on their own. Also, a woman who has not received an education is less informed regarding preventative health care practices, and as such she is more likely to experience an unwanted or unsafe pregnancy or to be exposed to sexually transmitted diseases (such as HIV) that undermine her ability to parent. The scenarios are endless. However, in each case, lack of education for women intensifies the already complicated situation.

While educational disparities perpetuate the orphan crisis, education can be powerfully leveraged to alleviate the orphan crisis. Educating a young woman not only transforms her life but also transforms her community. A young woman who receives education is better equipped to make empowered decisions about her life as well as to contribute to her community in meaningful ways. By providing access to education for girls, we can convey that girls are valuable, girls are worth investing in, and girls are powerful agents of change in their communities—girls matter. This message has implications for economic development, health care, and human rights. An educated young woman can provide an income to support her children. An educated young woman is better informed regarding responsible health and reproductive practices for her and her children. An educated young woman is more likely to understand her value and thus less likely to accept the cultural mores that promulgate abuse and regard women and children as property. From an economic perspective, educating women is smart; from a human perspective, educating women is essential to our work for social justice and the restoration of right relationships.

12. Ibid.

Education alone does not adequately address the orphan crisis. However, the orphan crisis cannot be wholly addressed without tackling educational disparities for girls in developing nations.

As an adoptive mother with a faith that is being transformed by the *whole* story, I am committed to increasing access to education for the world's most vulnerable—I will count my effort a success if I can help prevent one child from becoming orphaned, if I can help one birth mother to parent. As adoptive parents, we can begin in our own homes by placing a high value on education and its transformative value. However, we must not stop there. We must also invest in education. For example, consider how you can invest in education for vulnerable girls in your own community and in the world (volunteering, mentorship, and financial support). Organizations such as World Vision work to provide increased access to education both within the United States and around the world.[13] Consider helping alleviate the orphan crisis by partnering with World Vision or another organization with a similar mission.

Social Justice and Human Rights

Because of my personal investment in adoption, I seek to examine and understand social injustices that are contributing to the orphan crisis. And, on a more personal level, I attempt to grasp the issues of social injustice intertwined in my son's story. I do not have answers to all of my questions, but I would not be acknowledging my son's *whole* story if I did not ask the hard questions. What are the social issues that allow adoptive mothers to parent while birth mothers are not afforded the opportunity to parent? How do we move beyond working to alleviate the orphan crisis through adoption and toward working to prevent the orphan crisis? I believe there will always be situations in which adoption is necessary—and it is ultimately a beautiful act of God's love and grace for his children. However, is it really acceptable to advocate for adoption while turning our backs on the underlying causes of children without parents?

I recently found myself engaged in a riveting dialogue with my students—the question, posed by one particular student, was of the connection between culture and morality. Morality is, in part, determined by culture. For example, in some cultural contexts, making eye contact with an elder, blowing your nose in public, or dating more than one person before

---

13. World Vision, "Our Impact."

marriage is so offensive that it is considered to be morally wrong; in other cultures, these practices are not given a second thought, and certainly not considered to be morally wrong. Therefore, if we accept the premise that culture determines morality, then how can we take a stance that anything is in fact wrong? Or specifically, as my student queried, how could we ever look upon another cultural practice, determine it is wrong, and intervene to stop the practice? I was pleased that my student was thinking deeply about this issue—struggling with the very tension with which I too have struggled. I responded as I often do, encouraging my student to wrestle with the issue until she finds a stance that resonates with her spirit. However, believing that it is part of my role to offer guidance and my understanding of the truth, I also offered my perspective. Certainly, ways of being vary across cultures, and a behavior that is maladaptive, or perhaps considered morally wrong, in one culture may be an adaptive, or right, behavior in another culture. I may not always understand other ways of being, or even agree with them. However, difference alone neither necessitates nor justifies intervention on my part. Yet, not all cultural practices are merely representative of multiple ways of being. Instead, some cultural practices violate basic human rights and are issues of social justice where intervention is both justified and necessitated. Take, for example, the practice of female genital mutilation. You could argue that this is a cultural practice deeply rooted in traditional and cultural mores, a practice that simply cannot be understood outside of the culture. In fact, I would not argue with that stance—the practice is deeply rooted in tradition, and I do not understand it. However, I believe that intervention in a case such as female genital mutilation is necessary.

Female genital mutilation attacks a specific part of the female anatomy, causes severe, prolonged pain, and helps maintain a view of women and girls as not-quite-human. As a Christian, I do not accept the premise that morality is culturally bound to the point that it is void of any absolute truth of right and wrong or good and evil. Instead, as an act of love, care, and provision for God's children, we are commanded not only to love God but also to love one another. Social justice is ultimately a response to these commandments—to love the Lord our God and to love our neighbors. How can we love our neighbors, or be in right relationship with them, if we use our power or influence to threaten their existence, freedom, and basic sense of being human?

Like female genital mutilation, human rights violations further inflame the orphan crisis. Infringing a woman's human rights directly hinders her ability successfully to parent her children. For example, consider the young mother who is persecuted for her religious beliefs, forcibly removed from her home, and jailed. Her ability to parent before this event may have been feeble at best; now any hope of family preservation has been lost. Or consider the case of a mother who does not have access to food or clean water. Not only will she become malnourished and sick, but her children will be doubly victims: their parent may be made incapable of parenting, and they themselves may become malnourished both because of lack of parental care and because of unclean water. Finally, consider the case of young women who, by force, are enslaved in sexual trafficking. In the worst cases, their children too are forced into sexual slavery. Those who are lucky may be spared the firsthand trauma of sexual slavery, but nonetheless they are victims of sexual exploitation and abuse.

As an adoptive mother, citizen of my community, and a child of God, my desire is to advocate for human rights and work for social justice, thus exemplifying love for my neighbors. Recently, I have been impressed and inspired by the work of International Justice Mission (IJM), which advocates for and intervenes to uphold human rights and freedoms. Specifically, through victim relief, perpetrator accountability, survivor aftercare, and structural transformation, IJM leverages public justice systems to work for victims of abuse and oppression.[14] Yet, my theology also informs my worldview, and I know that all things cannot be made right or equal in the kingdom of the world. Despite our best efforts, evil will proliferate, human rights will be violated, and countless orphans will continue merely to exist in the margins of society. Only in the kingdom of God does God make all things right. But in the ultimate spirit of adoption, our adoption into God's heavenly, eternal family, and certainly in the spirit of God's transcending love for us, God's children, we must try to do better, becoming those who "do not merely listen to the word, and so deceive themselves. [But] do what it says" (Jas 1:22).

The question of what to do is one that we must all ask, prayerfully consider, and reflect upon in quiet moments of solitude. Furthermore, I do not believe that we are all called to the same action. Yet, through the work of God, all of our calls to action are in concert with one another and with the restorative power of God's love, redemption, and justice. My family has

---

14. International Justice Mission, "Who We Are."

been called to adopt a child internationally. While this is our story, God may be calling your family to adopt domestically or to provide much needed short-term foster care within your own community. In other cases, God may not be calling your family to adopt at all but rather to advocate for the orphan by working to alleviate poverty, address health care and education disparities, and promote social justice. In my own experience, embracing the *whole* story is an attempt to respond to God's call for my family, and I now more fully understand the heart of God for the poor, for the marginalized, for the orphan. We must each prayerfully consider the role that God is calling us to, reflect upon our respective gifts, talents, and resources, and embrace an openness to seeing ourselves as part of the problem—and, ultimately, come to embrace the loving, redemptive truth that we too are part of the solution.

12

The Fruitful Tree

DAVID MICHAEL HASLET

My brother and I were the first twins in ten years our adoption agency did not need to separate. While I can't remember when I first knew I was adopted, I can remember shock at learning about twins being given to different families when I was in my early adolescent years. "How many twins," I wondered, "are walking around living life not knowing there is someone else who could have been a best friend of theirs while growing up? How different their lives could have been!"

Timothy, my twin, was a best friend: one with whom to create intricate Lego worlds, pass footballs, and explore vacant lots through blackberry bracken walls. I don't remember talking all that much with Timothy in our growing-up years—but talk didn't seem profoundly necessary. More profound was simply time together. Though I had always known I was adopted, and though I strongly felt a part of my adoptive family, looking back, I am thankful I had the benefit of another in the same position as I—similar interests, similar curiosities, similar looks even. Perhaps looking similar to others in a family helps foster a sense of belonging.

I know it did for my adoptive mom, who dyed her hair to match our hair color when we were very young, though I believe she stopped after she and my adoptive dad brought home our younger sister, Adrianne, a fiery redhead with personality to match. Adrianne could get along warmly with anyone and everyone.

The Spirit of Adoption

We three children of the family didn't talk much about being adopted, perhaps because it did not seem unusual to us, and when, in conversation, others lifted eyebrows with "you're *adopted*?" questions, my surprise was with their surprise. Adoptive families seemed just as natural—I simply didn't *yet* know many others who were adopted.

I've come across some who found out sometime in their growing-up years that they were adopted, rather than before they could remember. My advice to prospective adoptive parents would be to follow my own parents' wisdom: tell adopted children before they can remember that they're adopted. This way avoids possible shock of the revelation and can start meaningful conversation about the nature of family. My mom's phrase was "though you're not children of my womb, you're children of my heart."

I took this to heart, feeling settled in my family, content to not look deeply into biological roots. Up until college years, my wondering about biological parents was only superficial, mostly along the lines of how tall I'd be or if I'd become bald (the answers being "fairly short" and "yes," though a beard makes up for the loss of hair on top). Being enamored with medieval history, I dreamed about being discovered as a long-lost relative in royal lineage. *And then, they'd find we're twins! It's a good thing I'm six minutes older!* I can also remember thinking in high school that when it came to dating, I shouldn't date anyone who looked too much like me, just in case we were related.

The answers to these questions, I knew, I would have a chance to discover when I turned eighteen. What I knew from closed adoption agency paperwork, beyond physical statistics and brief cultural heritage, was this: both biological father and mother were art professors.

Biographical information for my biological mother, while scant, was more complete than that for my biological father, leading me to guess that she was more involved in giving my brother and me for adoption. Significantly, she gave three stipulations to the adoption agency for prospective birth parents: 1) a belief in higher education; 2) a belief in a higher power; and 3) that the adoptive parents would expose my brother and me to the arts. My parents gratefully accepted and did their best to fulfill each of these requests. They first treated college as a natural continuation of high school, helping us greatly with the costs involved. Regular church attendance and mission trips to Native American reservations and to Tijuana to help with building projects began to orient my life with better focus. Not being artists, my parents fulfilled the third stipulation by bringing us to the Seattle

Children's Theatre throughout childhood. They exposed us to the occasional drawing or watercolor class in summers. Having a children's bookstore as the family business, we also had the opportunity to meet illustrators who visited the store for book signings, watching them draw pictures from their storybooks on the event room wall murals.

What agency paperwork didn't include was that our biological father, James, met our biological mother, Patricia, while they were both art professors at the same university. They knew each other only briefly, yet my brother and I came from the affair. James couldn't care for us—he had a wife, a daughter, and a son on the way. Patricia considered raising us by herself until she learned there were two babies. With strong support from family, she took care of us well, giving us away with love. We learned her parents were with her in the delivery room.

But my brother and I didn't know any of this at the time, of course. Why were we given away? Being a trusting person, I believe I naturally accepted that it was the right choice. I honestly can't remember feeling discarded, I'm thankful to say. Perhaps this is thanks to my parents' repeated encouragements: "Your biological mother loved you so much that she gave you to a family who could take care of you and love you as their own." While Timothy did at times feel rejected, I simply wondered if our birth mother wanted to contact us.

At eighteen years, my twin brother and I contacted the adoption agency, providing our contact information and expecting that our biological mother's contact information would be given to us. We found that the agency had no such information on record. That was the first time I can remember feeling slighted, and questions about the adoption surfaced with more poignancy.

However, college was beginning, and with it much that was new and challenging. I found myself engrossed in an exciting whirlwind of life, navigating a myriad of questions, fears, hopes, joys, and dreams that came from studies, relationships, and newfound faith. Largely focused as I was on the present and the future, the past became overshadowed. While questions about my biological parents subsided for me, they didn't subside for my twin brother, who attended the same university. His desire to find our biological parents seemed to deepen, culminating with a senior art project dealing with a sense of anger at the abandonment of adoption.

Our search at the time seemed thwarted, as our biological mother had not left her name or contact information, but Timothy wasn't dissuaded; he soon discovered that Oregon, the state in which we were adopted, had recently passed Measure 58, releasing original birth certificates to those adopted. Significantly, these certificates revealed birth parent names. By writing to the hospital in which we were born and to the delivering doctor, then, we were able to secure a copy of both original birth certificates, which included a name: Patricia.

With name in hand, we were able to link background information to continue the search. Remembering Patricia had been an art professor somewhere near Portland, Timothy began contacting university libraries for yearbooks with hopes of finding her picture. After the first positive match, librarians referred him to another university, as she'd only worked there (with James) for a year. The story was similar at the next university, which referred Timothy to the school where she had earned her master's degree. Once there, Timothy next filled out a lost friend/family form, checking the "family" box, and received her home address. We drafted a joint letter to send to our biological mother.

Her first response by letter: "Finally!" Somehow, her contact information had been misplaced by the adoption agency, and she had actually been waiting for us to contact her. In subsequent letters, Patricia mentioned the names of our biological father and his two children.

Not long after this, Timothy's wife, Elizabeth, found an article in which a young woman described her mother breastfeeding her infant brother, weeping with the news that her husband had had an affair and that the woman he had had an affair with was pregnant with twins. She knew the twins were given for adoption and wondered what became of them. Her name, Jacinda, was one of the names Patricia had given us. We emailed Jacinda, sending pictures, and what followed was a series of letters that can only be described as wonderfully redemptive.

This year, I enter my twelfth year of teaching art at a public high school. Art wasn't always a focus in life, though. When young, Timothy and I would often doodle, drawing space battles and designing castles on large rolls of butcher paper used at the family bookstore. In high school, though, as people often compare twins, he was the "artist."

My brother, Timothy, is a gifted painter. When his eldest daughter lost a stuffed purple hippo she treasured, Timothy painted her a replacement, one that shows such personality that others besides his daughter are endeared to the picture when they see it. He then began a business, painting treasured toys of childhood and calling it the Velveteen Hippo Project after his daughter's toy. Besides this, Timothy has been a part of plein air painting competitions and exhibitions on Whidbey Island, near Seattle.

To keep some kind of distinction when entering college, I decided to pursue a non-art major. It wasn't until I completed a minor in psychology that I discovered I really did enjoy things artistic and that I should pursue something in that field. I chose art administration, interning with museums in Washington State and San Francisco.

While good experience, it wasn't as I had envisioned. I decided upon a different track and took a job teaching English as a second language to children in China. There I discovered a love of teaching through what was a trial by fire in the truest sense. Baotou Iron and Steel, my new employer, ran perhaps half of the schools in the city of Baotou, and I was to teach classes supplementary to the school day—after school and on weekends. The only requirements were to be a native speaker and to have some kind of experience working with kids; amazingly, no teaching experience was required. After a number of emails with the teacher I was to replace—also a Whitworth University alumnus—I was offered the job.

My first two weeks were like living in a dream, feeling like I would awaken at any time, taking in the sights of crowded, dusty city streets, tiled buildings, the smells of restaurants, food carts, and waste piles upon sidewalks, and the sounds—vendors (apparently) calling out their wares, cars honking, and celebratory strings of fireworks setting off car alarms at midday. While my new boss, Mr. Liu, arranged classes, I explored my new home, walking through the streets, unable to read signage. I had taken a bit of Mandarin while in college, but everyone seemed to speak more quickly than I could understand. The food was wonderful, but oh, how my forearm ached from constant chopstick use!

My many students were shy at first but determined, quick to laugh, and willing to make mistakes. I had never taught before, apart from a few Sunday school lessons, and as I fumbled through planning and delivering lessons—sometimes using an established curriculum, sometimes complementing with other activities—I found joy in the challenge and the interaction with students. I learned quickly because I needed to. With my youngest students, seven years of age, I led English word games with the help of a translator, and with my oldest students, seventeen years of age, I read (and acted) from *Charlie and the Chocolate Factory*. "The Prince of Pondicherry lived in a *chocolate* castle? Did we hear him correctly?" students asked each other. I drew a fair number of illustrations while telling stories and answering questions. What discussions we had!

I can remember also teaching tongue twisters. After I challenged my students ("a proper copper coffee pot" was a good starter), they challenged me with tongue twisters in Mandarin. I told them of stories like *Sir Gawain and the Green Knight* and they responded by telling me, in English, about the Monkey King. Watching the theater as a child improved my teaching, reminding me to project as an actor would and communicate with body language and expression. To foster hospitality and community, I joined others for large dinners almost weekly. During the first dinner, one of my colleague's adult students stood and sang for everyone. I assumed she was a singer by trade until the person next to her stood to sing, and then the person next to him . . . "What? I need to stand up and serenade everyone?" I asked. In answer, faces smiled and nodded emphatically. Thankfully, Irish ballads weren't too well known or too out of place.

What developed within me was a love for the vocation. Returning to the United States, I enrolled in a master's in teaching program at Whitworth University and soon began a career as a high school art teacher. My first job was in rural Alaska, teaching in two Yup'ik Eskimo villages. "Everything will be provided for you—even your home! You won't even need a pancake flipper!" said the recruiter at the job fair for teachers I attended. The half single-wide mobile homes reserved for itinerant teachers were in disrepair, with well-used lightweight door handles, tubs lined with either brown or blue stains, gaps around doors, and particle wood shelving. When I noticed I didn't have a kitchen knife, I gratefully found one embedded in a wall while scouting the "old school" of the village. My kitchen was now complete.

Mobile homes are meant to be light to meet road restriction requirements, but no roads led to the two villages where I taught. Likely, my home had come by barge before winter's onset years before. Alaska in winter is dark, and while I was befriended by local families, the persistent darkness added to my feeling of isolation. A care package sent from friends included candles—something I hadn't thought much of previously but came to treasure for their warmth and living light. I read and prayed by these lights.

After school hours, I often went for long walks on four-wheeler tracks outside the village. Within minutes, I felt again within the wild, sometimes seeing pheasants, in vibrant greens and reds, perched atop stumps, sometimes seeing moose mulling around pebble-banked rivers. Freshets and soft tundra ground with few alpine-like trees completed my surroundings, and I would wander, wading at times with my knee-high rubber boots, hearing sounds of water, wind, and raven-call.

On one such walk, I wandered farther than usual from my home village of New Stuyahok. Cresting a hill, I looked down, admiring the view, and noticed movement in bushes perhaps fifty yards away. Spiked brown fur, perhaps as tall as me, moved back and forth—fur lighter in color than moose I'd seen. Only the shoulder hump and back of the brown bear were visible.

Thoughts blazed through my head of a local man telling me that bears can run up to forty miles per hour. With their heads bobbing up and down at full speed, a shot is difficult and must be made to the weak spot: the collarbone. What would I do if it saw me? I wondered. I didn't have a gun! I've shot through cans a few times with .22s, but never anything like a charging bear. I ran, trying to keep my boots on through mud as I sprinted for home. The next day, I returned to the spot with another teacher by four-wheeler to see deep bear prints and broken branches—proof to another and myself that my story was true.

It was in this wild and isolated setting that I corresponded with my half-sister from my biological father's side. Jacinda shared with my brother and me a love of travel and art. We exchanged accounts of journeys to distant lands to explore and experience cultures, and of how the places we live help shape our lives—she wrote of New Zealand, I wrote of Alaska and China. She wrote, too, about her love of photography, and of being a university professor, and of memories growing up with our biological father and half-brother, who, incidentally, is a sculptor. Discovering shared interests and talents with newfound family while being so far away from family became a surprise joy.

Our contact with biological family brought further connections to light. Patricia married a kung fu master, and as my wife and I teach tae kwon do, we traded stories about similarities and differences in the disciplines. They have a son, and he, Timothy, and I share an interest in soccer. James' mother loved languages and growing blueberries, as I do, and Patricia's father shared a love of singing—he was even part of a barbershop quartet.

After Patricia's father died, she looked through his belongings and found a family album with a picture of my brother and me in it—one we had sent to Patricia of him playing a tin whistle and I an Irish drum. It was the first picture we sent to her after making contact. Hearing he kept this picture brought a sense of loss over grandparents we never knew but who still considered us part of the family.

We chose a city park at my home in rural California for our first meeting with Patricia, her husband, son, and sister. Imagine a square green field—the kind used casually for kickball or water balloon tosses—surrounded by pine trees, picnic benches, and suburban streets, all under inland West Coast summer sun. We figured it was a neutral setting that in fine weather would be conducive to casual strolls or seated talks. The park was large enough, however, that when we saw each other we were on opposite sides of the field. Unsure we spotted the correct family, we unintentionally lined up, both sides, and slowly walked towards each other, meeting in the middle of the field with hesitant yet sincere smiles and some handshakes, expressing relief at having found each other. Something about movement, something about expression and personality identified us, and, more observing than talking, we began to reiterate and build upon what we had shared in letters.

We were also able to meet with our biological father, James, along with Jacinda, at an ice cream shop in the town in which we grew up, beginning conversations that, though halting at first, were imbued with a mysterious affinity. "My hands look just like his," Timothy told me afterwards. At each meeting with newfound blood relatives, brothers, aunts, and cousins, I found myself struck by likenesses in looks and personality. "When I met Patricia," my wife later told me, "I knew right away where your peaceable demeanor comes from." There was a sense of instant kinship.

However, as much as the biological side shares looks and interests, the bond (at least yet) isn't as strong as with the family with whom I was raised. When it comes down to it, we're Haslets. Our memories of our formative years have helped forge the sense of a greater immediacy within our adoptive family. My adoptive parents did not simply play a substitutionary role. They became our parents. What is family, then? How can blood connections and adoptive connections be compared? Is one as valid or more valid than the other?

My wife (who doesn't look too much like me) also has experience with adoption, having two older, adopted twin sisters. Coral grew up estranged from her father, calling him her biological father as a way to distinguish him from her later stepfather. "How can I call him my father when I don't even know him?" she asks. Fatherhood is lineage, and more than this.

When my parents first moved up to the Seattle area from Portland with my twin and me (though not yet my sister), neighbors of ours became like family. Fran, especially, became like a grandmother to us, and on many occasions, talking over brunch on Sundays, we half-joked about how we adopted her into our family. It was Fran who made food from scratch—gingersnaps and apricot, plum, and lemon bars. It was Fran who convinced Adrianne that she made even the sugar cubes we sucked on when we thought no one was looking. We picked raspberries in her backyard and played fetch with pinecones and a neighbor's black lab. It was Fran who taught me about forgiveness after I broke a bedroom window with a failed three-point shot from beyond the driveway to the house-mounted hoop. As my parents' parents didn't live nearby, Fran became our grandma, in effect, even more than those whom we knew by that name. We loved our grandparents, but we shared life together with our Grandma Fran.

My four-year-old son, sitting next to me as I write, asks what I am writing about. "I am writing about how Uncle Tim and Aunt Adrianne and I were adopted," I say. "What's 'adopted'?" he asks. I tell him how our parents were not able to take care of us and how Nana and Pops (my mom and dad) were not able to have children of their own. They prayed to God to be able to have children, and God, who loves us so much and takes care of us, gave us to Nana and Pops to be their children. My son's response: "They must have been *so happy*."

And he's right. Having come to believe in a loving God, I am convinced of his providing like a father. I am thankful not to have been aborted and for the thoughtfulness and care my biological mother showed my twin brother and me before we were born. I am thankful my parents' prayers were answered when they asked for twins (albeit twin girls), then a daughter. I am thankful for a neighbor who became a grandmother. Truly, "God sets the lonely in families" (Ps 68:6).

An avid gardener, I write looking out the back window of our house at our plots of vegetables and fruit trees. All are young and most are in containers, bearing small, much anticipated harvests. Some trees we have begun to prune in the espalier style, spread fanlike against fences, in order to face the sun and to be accessible for picking. Others are clumped together as a way to minimize tree growth and create a cluster of differing fruit.

The Spirit of Adoption

Our biggest specimen tree, however, is a combination tree that some call a fruit cocktail—a tree with various graftings that make a harmonious whole. Ours has two peach varieties with plum branches intermingling, creating an infusion of differently colored blossoms in spring and differently colored fruit through summer. Peaches, plums, and apricots, being of the *prunus* family, botanically, have this advantage of being able to be grafted in such a way in order to become something greater by blending branches.

Such is my family: the adoptive family in which I was raised, with connections by blood to my extended family, the good fruit of which continues to my immediate family today and future generations. I can't imagine what my family would be without my gregarious sister or parents. God provided in such a way that it would be so, and it is good.

And we love this family tree, filled with variety, which, though branches sometimes vie for space, at its best creates a harmonious whole. In giving us life and placing us with our adoptive family, then as adults reuniting us with our extended, blood family, God has brought something redemptive from the ugly situation of our conception. We are a part of a greater story of restoration, and knowing this lends hope in everyday living. Future difficulties and mistakes can also be redeemed. We love this evolving story we are a part of so much that my wife and I, after the births of two wondrous biological children, are considering building our family further through adoption.

God unites people in just such a way, bringing together all kinds of people from all over the world to inherit "life in the fullest," saying, "I will be a [parent] to you, and you will be my sons and daughters" (2 Cor 6:18). Such familial identity changes *everything,* enabling us to live beyond our potential, through the Spirit as members of a larger body. We know that we have and will have all that we need, having been told by Jesus, "do not worry about your life, . . . Look at the birds of the air; they do not sow or reap or store away in barns, and yet your heavenly Father feeds them. Are you not much more valuable than they?" (Matt 6:25a, 26). God took care of us when we needed family, giving us more of a family than we could have envisioned—rich and varied.

13

Adoption of Lizette

Moses Harris

"Just because you are a preacher does not mean that you will make a good parent." These were the first words the social worker said to me during our initial home visit. Instead of speaking to me and my wife, Ruby, in a polite, conventional manner, this individual, not having had any previous relationship with us, began the meeting with an *ad hominem* perspective. I am not sure what he hoped to accomplish by such a statement, but his opening words etched themselves indelibly in my mind.

Adoption for Our Family

Adoption means to take another's child and bring it up as one's own.[1] Before we adopted Lizette, we cared for many children at various stages of our married life, without the legal part, and we treated them as if they were our own. My wife and I never had any biological offspring, but since she always wanted a large family (she hoped to have eight children), she constantly extended her love and her resources to children who needed a mother's touch. First of all, we kept B and J. Their mother brought them to visit us one day, and when she left she said that she was leaving her children with us. Instant parents. Ruby also provided for the twins, M and M1, as their parents lived for a while in our home. Since the twins were not even two

---

1. *Concise Oxford English Dictionary*, s.v. "adoption."

years old, she loved feeding them and changing their diapers and dressing them and putting three dozen barrettes into M's hair. At one point we kept M2 and S for a short period of time.

And then there's N. At nine months of age his mother allowed us to keep him as if he were our own. He stayed in our home. He went with us to church. He ran with us on the beach. He ate with us in restaurants. When he was three and a half years old, his mother sent word that she was pregnant with another child and that if we did not take her second child as our own, then she would remove N from our care. Ruby was not ready to raise two children, so we made the painful decision of giving him back to his mother. The pain of losing him was intense. It was as if someone reached into my chest cavity, grabbed my heart, and yanked it out. It was like the scene in *El Cid* when he was about to leave his wife and his daughters—like separating the fingernail from the finger. It was a mother's yearning for her only child taking flight on a one-way journey. It was a father's emotional distress at losing a son with unlimited potential.

A Bit of Stacy's History

We kept Stacy, Lizette's deceased birth mother, for a brief period of time. Stacy was Ruby's niece, and in her teenage years she came to spend several months with us, during which she celebrated her sixteenth birthday. Shortly afterwards, Stacy returned to southern California, and we really did not have much contact with her.

Stacy had a difficult childhood, often without the presence of her father, and she, her siblings, and her mother lived in the projects. One negative event in Stacy's life was the theft of her bed while they were in this housing complex, and the memory of this burglary bothered her for quite some time. Stacy's mother is to be commended because she did not allow this environment to dictate a negative future for herself and for her family. While serving as a single parent for her three children, Stacy's mother earned both a BA and an MA from top U.S. universities.

As of this writing, I have many standout thoughts about Stacy. She did not mind working. In fact, she took pride in being gainfully employed, and she worked at different jobs, one being in a restaurant. She loved life, and she had a sense of humor. She asked me once, "What do you get when you cross an elephant with a rhinoceros?" Her answer, "Eliphino." Stacy chose to get married on the 4th of July. Why? She wanted lots of fireworks on that day.

Stacy married Big Mike, and they gave birth to Little Mike, Lizette's older brother. Big Mike is now deceased, and Little Mike, who is not little anymore, is twenty-four. Since these siblings live in different states, they see each other only every two years or so. Lizette loves Little Mike, and she fawns all over him when she is in his presence.

Stacy made some choices—I am not sure of the details—that led to her premature death at the age of thirty-five. Ruby and I went to California when she died; I did the eulogy. We decided that we did not want her beautiful two-and-a-half-year-old daughter caught up in the "system." As you probably have determined, our daughter Lizette is Ruby's great-niece by biology. After losing N and others, we decided that we would go through legal adoption if we ever took oversight for anyone else. We obtained permission to bring Lizette back to Washington State, where we completed the lengthy, painstaking, and often infuriating process of adoption.

Did I just say lengthy? Yes I did. Ruby and I attended thirty hours of instruction on the process of adoption. We responded to more than fifty essay questions, each on about what it means to be a parent. We attended CPR classes. We underwent numerous home visits by individuals representing the state of Washington. We made dozens and dozens and dozens of calls, some of which went unanswered for months because the area code of the region of California we were calling had changed, and our calls regarding Lizette's adoption did not make it to the intended recipient for almost a year. In fact, we know that it is because of God that we now have Lizette as our legally adopted daughter. Because of this area code glitch, the social worker attending our case had not heard from us, and she decided that we were no longer interested in adopting Lizette.

Did I just say lengthy? We met weekly for prayer with the president and faculty and staff of the university where I work. They prayed consistently for more than a year for the adoption to go through, not knowing at the time that not even our telephone messages were getting through.

Did I say lengthy again? Every process has a beginning, a middle, and an end. However, this adoption procedure seemed as if it would never come to completion. We were in our early to late fifties when we brought Lizette into our home, and we had to listen to lectures on parenting skills from individuals who had no children of their own and who were half our age. The procedure was quite protracted, but in the end we prevailed.

The Spirit of Adoption

"And as I close." This phrase is a commonplace among many preachers in the African-American community. The organ provides musical accompaniment for the speaker of the hour while the audience engages in an antiphonal response. A crescendo that was building for the last several minutes comes to completion.

"And as I close." My wife tells me sometimes that we preachers project several false cadences—"my final Scripture," "as I go to my seat," and "my last remark" being some of the "lies" that we tell as we come to the end of our sermon. My response to her is that we have many doors to close.

I mention preachers and individuals and cultures of African descent because my wife and Lizette and I are seen as African-Americans. Actually, we all have a significant percentage of Native American blood in us as well. I refer to the African-American culture because adoptions of our children have brought numerous challenges. I will mention three of them.

First of all, when cultures intersect, no one can continue with the traditional, time-worn, daily routines. What is taboo in one culture is acceptable in another, and vice versa. Multiple practices for adherents of either value system should be considered with a rational state of mind, and if these customs are not valid for the adopting family, then the adopting parents must be willing to say, "That was then, but this is now." If someone in a large city—this actually happened to a Caucasian female friend of our family—says that your biracial child has been out in the sun too long, then you need to esteem and to value that child regardless of the attitudes, the statements, and even the stares of those who are part of the majority culture.

Secondly, proper hair care and skin care are not impossible tasks for children of African descent. The hair texture of many African-Americans is often compared to lamb's wool. Consequently, children with a "different" grade of hair need special attention. Usually, this kind of hair only needs to be washed every seven to ten days because of dry scalp. After washing the child's hair, parents should apply oil to the scalp. In metropolitan areas, one can easily find a "black" barber or a "black" hairdresser. I put the "black" in quotes because even in college I had barbers who did not know how to cut my kind of hair. I eventually came across an individual from the Philippines who did a great job of giving me a haircut. And don't mention "ashy skin." Our darker-skinned children turn a pale grey when they get out of the shower or out of the swimming pool. We get rid of the "ash" by applying the proper kind of lotion or baby oil, usually found in the ethnic section of many of our national chain stores. A little dab, sometimes a bigger one applied over the entire body, will do the trick. Goodbye "ash."

Finally, our adopted children need to know that they are "black." We have raised our daughter, now a lovely developing teenager, on a need-to-know basis. We have withheld some teachings against racism and sexism and other biases within our society until we felt we had a "teachable moment." We would rather not have to engage in these discussions, but we do not want her to be unaware of current attitudes toward those who are racially or ethnically different. Moreover, knowing African-American history is an important part of knowing and understanding her identity. Now, for my "final closing."

After retaining an attorney to complete the paperwork for adoption, the day finally arrived when Lizette would become a permanent part of our family. Lizette, Ruby, and I, with our legal counsel, appeared before the judge in the adoption court. He and his staff were pleasant, and they were almost as exuberant as we were for the outcome of the adoption.

As of this writing Ruby and I have been married for forty seven and a half years. We are now in our late sixties, and Lizette has just celebrated her fifteenth birthday. She has a strong Christian worldview, she is an outstanding artist, and she loves to debate. We don't know what the future holds for her, but we are encouraging her to be all that she can be. She has brought great joy to our lives, establishing us as the family that we so long desired.

14

Love or Luck?

Douglas Webster

Friday night was our date night. Virginia was working two jobs to put me through doctoral studies at St. Michael's College in Toronto. We were virtually hand-to-mouth poor, but on Friday night we splurged. We routinely rendezvoused at our one-bedroom apartment at Steeles and Bathurst and then headed to Swiss Chalet for their rotisserie roasted chicken sandwich, the cheapest thing on the menu. After a long, hot, midsummer workweek, we gave ourselves permission to crash. We were about to leave, the key was in the door, when the phone rang. I remember looking at Virginia, as if to say, "Do we have to get that?" Her face said without words, "Might as well." I somewhat begrudgingly got to the phone on the fourth ring.

"Where have you been? I have been trying to get you all week!" The recognizable voice on the other end was our social worker, Ms. Cadbury, a fifty-something, grandmotherly type who wore bobby socks and worked for the Toronto Children's Aid Society. She had endeared herself to us during the official home-study when she described our hall closet, where we planned to remove the door and squeeze in a crib, as a cute baby alcove. We knew then that she was on our side.

On the phone Ms. Cadbury sounded a bit provoked and a little frantic. This was before the ubiquitous cell phone. Throughout the week, we were hardly ever home, making us even harder to reach.

"This was the last time I was going to call you before moving on to the next name on my list," she said, adding, "I have a baby for you." If we had known that we were anywhere near to the next on the list, we would have missed work and sat by the phone impatiently waiting. We had no idea we were even close. We had purposely determined not to get too excited because the adoption agency had said it could take another six months. I must have said, "Sorry," but I'm not sure. I was stunned. Staccato thoughts drummed through my mind. A Baby. Our Baby. Last call. Move on to the next on the list. I was suddenly bombarded by simple monosyllables. Reality had shifted under my feet. How could such complexity be described with so few words and such simple words at that?

Before I could say another word, she said, "You can pick up your son tomorrow at Women's College Hospital. Congratulations." She explained where and when to meet her at the hospital. She repeated her congratulations and said goodbye. We were probably her last order of business for the day. She could go home now. I hung up the phone. How does one tell his wife, who is waiting by the door, tired and hungry for a Swiss Chalet chicken sandwich, that life has just forever changed, that the earth's orbit froze for a moment? How do you say, "Our three-day-old baby boy, Jeremiah, is downtown and can be picked up in the morning?" In three minutes, five minutes max, from the time the key was in the door to the phone call, followed by my halting explanation, we both sat down stunned. Incredibly excited, grateful, and totally nervous all at the same time.

That night was a blur. I think I was in shock. I know we headed to Sears and spent ninety dollars on a crib mattress and a baby outfit in which to bring our son home from the hospital. We had purposely not filled the apartment with baby things so as not to get too excited too soon. But now we were playing catch-up. Neither of us slept much that night. We got on the phone and got our family equally excited, but not nearly as nervous. We were far from family and very much on our own. We may have been the most unprepared, naive parents on the face of the earth; at least that's how I felt.

We contemplated adoption even before we were married. At the age of eighteen I was diagnosed with non-Hodgkin Lymphoma. My cancer was first discovered due to a testicular tumor. The surgeons said there was a good chance I wouldn't be able to have children. Years later, when our relationship became serious, I remember telling Virginia. She took the news in stride, but when she told her mother and sister, they cried for hours. We entered into marriage half-hoping that the doctors got it wrong and that Virginia would become pregnant. But adoption was always in our minds as a real possibility.

After we moved to Toronto to do doctoral work, we began to talk and pray about having a family. Although more than thirty years have passed, we both remember vividly a conversation we had with a leading Toronto fertility expert. Before our visit with the specialist, we discussed the possible options. Virginia and I agreed that artificial insemination with the husband's sperm (AIH) was a biblically acceptable medical procedure. This involved harvesting my sperm, if that were possible, and inseminating Virginia. When the doctor learned that we were not open to donor artificial insemination (AID), he became angry. He turned to Virginia and said, "If you do not allow yourself to become pregnant, you will grow to resent this man and eventually hate him. I can give you want you want. Do you want to become pregnant or not?" Virginia looked at me, looked at him, and we excused ourselves. We got out of his office as fast as we could.

Looking back, I marvel at how the Lord led us along a winding path of soul-searching and waiting. The Lord gave us the determination to see it through, to fill out the applications, to go through the interviews at Toronto Children's Aid and other adoption agencies, and through it all to trust in his sovereignty. We both came from great families, and we wanted to share in that experience as parents. To seek the blessing of children seemed only natural, even if in our case we needed a special grace. I never thought we were "rescuing" a baby or giving a child a different life from what he or she might have had otherwise. We wanted to love our children the way we were loved, the way our parents had loved us, the way Christ loves us. This desire to have children and this love for our children remains such a deeply spiritual reality that I don't want to spiritualize it.

Ms. Cadbury's phone call hadn't actually traumatized me, but it came pretty close. By the time Andrew came along, a year and a half after Jeremiah, we were veterans. Andrew arrived earlier than we had anticipated as well, but by now we were prepared. He was born in Ottawa and delivered to our apartment by a Christian couple. I remember their handing him over to us. That sacred moment is forever etched in my memory. He was dressed in yellow and white and his face wore a contented grin. He is thirty now, and he risks his life as an ocean lifeguard in Dominical, Costa Rica, but he still wears that beautiful, contented grin I first saw when he was a week old. Our third child, Kennerly, arrived at the end of nine months of splendid anticipation. Surprise! She was the one who proved that we had been real parents all along. Adoption and conception are different, but it makes no difference in the heart of the parent. Either way, parents hold their children in their hearts.

By the time the third child arrives, parents are pretty relaxed about the whole thing, but with our first child we were anything but relaxed. That almost-missed call from Ms. Cadbury still makes me shiver. What if we had ignored the ring, waved it off, turned the key, and headed for dinner? We could have been staring blankly at each other over a chicken sandwich wondering if and when the adoption agency would give us a call. I say that because our conversation often turned to adoption and children after an exhausting week of study and work. To think that we almost missed our future is still unnerving to me. Ms. Cadbury meant it when she said that was her last try before moving down the list. We came perilously close to losing our firstborn son. Our son could have gone to another family. Of course, then he would not have been our firstborn son. As it turned out, all three of our children are firstborn, which is how I think the sons and daughters of God are privileged in the Gospel of the Kingdom.

At the appointed time, we arrived at the hospital, found the unit, and signed in. Frankly, I don't remember anything else, except that we were ushered into a small room with a very large Jamaican-born nurse hovering over a baby who was wailing and flailing with all his might. She was changing his diaper, and he was protesting with every single cell of his tiny little body. His whole body was red with anger. He was one unhappy camper, but his screaming subsided when he was changed and wrapped in a blanket and Virginia took him in her arms. His biological mother gave him the name Adam, a kind of placeholder until we could give him his real name. She named him well. He is after all, like us, a son of Adam. But we named him Jeremiah, believing that what the Lord said to the ancient prophet was true of our newborn son: "Before I formed you in the womb I knew you" (Jer 1:5).

Were we lucky? A few minutes later and we would have missed our social worker's call. She said it was her last try. She was about to call the next person on her list. Is Jeremiah our son because of a lucky turn of fate? Or does Divine Love prevail in spite of and in the midst of the vicissitudes of random circumstances and just-in-time phone calls? The Apostle Paul's confidence in our Heavenly Father makes sense to me: "In love he predestined us for adoption to sonship through Jesus Christ" (Eph 1:5). The language is truly breathtaking. Life is not a matter of lucky breaks. Life is by Divine design. My very own family is a redemptive analogy for my—for our—relationship to Christ. "For he chose us in him before the creation of the world to be holy and blameless in his sight" (Eph 1:4). Amen.

15

All Shall Be Well

Jeremiah Webster

> For no one is cast off by the Lord forever. Though he brings grief,
> he will show compassion, so great is his unfailing love.
> For he does not willingly bring affliction or grief to anyone.
>
> Lamentations 3:31–33

Letter

"At the time I'm writing this you have just been born." I was twenty and had just discovered a letter from my birth mother buried in a file cabinet. My mother, the one who had adopted me newborn, the one whose love transcended kin, the one I knew, had asked me to reorganize the files, their manila envelopes dog-eared, tattered, as old as I was. The letter was typed, `Courier`, on cheap office paper and resided between income tax returns and warranty agreements. Was I supposed to be seeing this? I wasn't sure. My adoption had never been a secret. My parents had been open, celebratory. My childhood was no great pathos. But a letter had never been mentioned, and I felt a strange sense of guilt for having found it.

Like a Jefferson Bible, the Webster narrative had just been revised.

The Spirit of Adoption

The letter relayed the events surrounding my conception, by turns both tragic and mundane. My daydreams would never again see birth parents jet-setting to the Riviera or touring the American Southwest with Hunter S. Thompson on a mescaline high. There was no miraculous birth, Templar bloodline, or revelation that I was in fact the bastard son of traveling thespians. I was a late-seventies evening shag between college students. I was exasperated panic weeks later. I was my father's indignation. I was a reason they stopped seeing each other.

"`He is a kind man,`" my mother wrote, "`but he is a man and so he has faults like any other...we could never get along without making eachother` [sic] `unhappy.`" She was working in a bookstore to pay for school when I was born. Her letter described life in Toronto during the summer of '79 and was deeply philosophical, sadness coupled with a mother's hope for her son: "`I am at fault...the risk of your happiness and mine is great.`" Had she kept me, she explained, I would have been a nine-to-five day care candidate. Had she kept me, "`we would have been miserable.`"

The letter wasn't all dross. It told me that my father had been in a band and sang in church. It explained that my mother was studying English literature at the university. Both of them shared a love for books and music. "`Your father wants to go on with his education perhaps to become a university professor.`" Anyone who knows me would recognize how intrinsic these disciplines are to my own identity. I grew up in a supportive family, a family committed to the arts, to faith in Christ, but I was struck by how innately I had followed the path of my biological parents. There was kinship between strangers. Until the file cabinet discovery, there had been no way to see that.

My mother's letter established an undeniable connection between who I was at twenty and who I had been in utero. My birth became history, like the Peloponnesian War (431 BC) or the first issue of Bob Kane's *Batman* (AD 1940), a welcome alternative to the prenatal phantoms I had been forced to conjure. I wonder, even now, if the hands that had typed this note held me newborn. I wonder if my father had been at the hospital. I wonder if siblings are drinking coffee, reading books, and raising children in an age of terror and triviality, as I am. Finding the letter prompted interest in contacting my biological family, but I never pursued it. The letter emigrated from my parents' files to my own when I moved out. Fourteen years passed and I did nothing.

Now I read it all the time.

Two Loves

One of the earliest stories I heard as a child was the Judgment of Solomon. My family owned a fifties-era, R-rated illustrated-Bible. Jezebel really looked like a whore, Saul's eyes flashed with macho-demonic rage, and Christ's passion left little to the imagination. The painting that accompanied the third chapter of 1 Kings had Solomon holding a Midwest-Anglo baby high above his head, sword ready to split the infant in two. Peacocks swaggered around the throne. A jungle cat reclined like a sphinx. The attendants were wide-eyed bureaucrats, infanticide junkies. The child's mouth mimicked Munch's scream. It haunted me for years.

In the narrative, two women give birth to healthy infants. During a night of restless sleep, one of the mothers accidentally smothers the newborn lying next to her. An ensuing maternity dispute over the surviving child brings the women before Solomon's court. In his wisdom, the king proposes cutting the babe in half and dividing it between them.

"Put blood on the rug," one replies.

"Spare the child. Give it to her," the other insists.

"The true mother," Solomon declares, "is the latter."

෴ ෴ ෴

This story was so familiar, so ready-made for the Sunday school flannel boards of my youth, that I failed to see its parallel with my adoption until I became a parent. I remember where I was (Ubiquitous Coffee Shop, 108th St.), the time (10:32 AM), and even the weather (Seattle Noir), the moment I thought . . . *That's her. That's what my mom did. I Kings 3:26. And that's why I exist.* The once-hidden resolve of my biological mother found definition in a biblical narrative. Solomon recognized that authentic love always sacrifices for the beloved. A true mother, beyond an elusive quest for fairness, beyond genetic right, beyond the experience of parenthood, makes sure her baby is safe. In the presence of one woman seeking possession while the other demanded protection, Solomon's verdict was plain.

It's easy to privilege relationships of mutual benefit and self-actualization. Our culture readily endorses this brand of idolatry. *Eros* fixation abandons marriage when it lacks convenience, seeks orgasm like the Holy Grail, and resents children when they fail as immortality symbols. The phrase

The Spirit of Adoption

"What happens in Vegas, stays in Vegas" has transcended PR campaigns to become a way of life. This is why my mother's choice was so compelling. It was a defiant "No!" in an age questing after Tom Wolfe's "Master of the Universe"—that ruthless eighties libertine both emulated and envied. Her decision to *keep the baby*, not for herself, but so that he would "`grow up and experience all the things in this huge world even when this means sorrow and pain`," embodied the highest regard for human life I can imagine. For my mother, the *potentiality* of my birth was reason enough.

I've never liked the phrase "giving up the child for adoption." The syntax alone is impulsive, like "giving up the neglected jet ski," or "giving up reality television for Lent." There is sacrifice involved, sure, but nothing of real gravitas. Having experienced firsthand a parent's zeal for his or her child, the *I would drink poison* fervor, I can't imagine the self-denial my mother possessed during the months she carried me. It would have required the full support of family, infinite fortitude, and some measure of faith. Faith that an adoption agency would find a loving home, faith in "`the ways of the world which are larger and more mysterious than either you or I can understand`," faith that the inevitable grief would heal. As I've cared for my son Liam during the past few years, I've tried to imagine nine months of waiting only to return to a silent apartment, an entire night of sleep available, the illumination of a child's birth removed like the flip of a switch. I admire this stranger, this mother before Solomon, who chose love in an age that cannot reconcile the *autonomy of self* with the *death of self* that children require.

It took Liam's birth to realize I had been the recipient of two loves. There was the love of a mother who chose adoption, even when it meant severing motherhood along with the umbilical cord. There were young parents who had prayed for a son they couldn't have and who emphatically welcomed me as their own. This economy of grace is beyond understanding, and it is tragic that a stigma toward adoption persists. The fastest way to suck air from a room, to inflict dread on a church potluck, was to announce my origins. There were times I'm certain my brother (also adopted) brought up the subject just to spite guests who were staying too long at the Webster dinner table. It elicited pained stares, like having three eyes in a world of two or being the last of an endangered species on public display. This attitude denied love an opportunity for cultivation, for definition beyond a predictable list of appetites, and undermined the radical love of my parents, who treat me more like a firstborn son than any kinship of mere biology. When we resign adoption to the second tier, to the *unfortunate class*, we become the antithesis of Solomon's Judgment. We raise the love of the possible above our heads, wait for a cry of protest, and when there is none, we run it through.

∽ ∽ ∽

I started writing a letter for Liam. This was in the hospital, as he slept like an unblemished god in a bedside crib. It began just as my birth mother's had: "At the time I am writing this you have just been born." There in the dark, as Liam and Kristin slept, I wrote the sentence on hospital letterhead. Well-meaning friends and family members had told Kristin and me to do this sort of thing. "He'll grow up fast," they said. "You'll regret not having the memories."

But I never finished it. I couldn't progress past that first line. There were too many diapers, too many appointments, too many midnight zombie reenactments, too many severities to a person's sanity. The newborn-parent sequence had no room for contemplation. If I had finished it on the day of Liam's birth, it would have affirmed the primal love Kristin and I had for him. It would have mentioned the moment of total recognition when I saw his face. It would have told him we cried ourselves blind as Kristin held his impossible smallness to her breast. It would have told him secret prayers. It would have told him we weren't going anywhere.

Fire and Rose Are One

Christianity is all paradox. To follow Christ is to embrace a living tension. God is one in three. Immortal souls reside in mortal frames. We are enemies of the divine. We are coheirs with Christ. To live, we must be willing to die. I can only explain how an unwanted pregnancy merited celebration, or how two vastly different manifestations of love made my life possible, through a Christian understanding of God's nature. Oppositions worked in concert. Acts of providence preceded my awareness of them.

Few authors understand this tension as well as T. S. Eliot. To read Eliot's poetry is to be in the presence of a paradoxical mind, whether it be the coffee spoons of Prufrock, the triune *shantih* of *The Waste Land*, the alien gods of the Magi, or the prophetic bird of *Four Quartets*. It is this latter poem that has provided the most counsel as I've reflected on my birth and adoption. I resonate deeply with the pilgrimage Eliot describes, especially in the poem's final section, "Little Gidding." It is a powerful metaphor for the tensions that surrounded my adoption.

The last stanza begins with a memorable declaration:

> We shall not cease from exploration
> And the end of all our exploring
> Will be to arrive where we started
> And know the place for the first time.[1]

The rhapsody of these lines recalls the epigraph in *Four Quartets* from Heraclitus: "The way up and the way down are one and the same." Self-understanding is not as linear as time might suggest. Knowledge ebbs, lies dormant, and in rare cases startles us with an immediate revelatory power. To know thyself (as the ancient Greeks advised) is a lotus of enlightenment. It is also a source of ennui. "To arrive where we started / And know the place for the first time" captures the admiration and sorrow I have for my biological mother, but I had to experience a lifetime of commitment from my parents, marriage, and fatherhood before this level of empathy was even possible. I had to reside fully in the role of son, husband, and father before I could recognize the unmerited inheritance of my adoption.

"Little Gidding" ends with a phrase from Julian of Norwich: "And all shall be well, and / All manner of thing shall be well."[2] This hopeful refrain is complicated by what follows: "When the tongues of flame are in-folded / Into the crowned knot of fire / And the fire and the rose are one."[3] Eliot's imagery suggests the fire of God's Holy Spirit (the "Comforter" of John 16:7 and Pentecost) even as it recalls the fire of Dante's final trial in *The Divine Comedy*. The journey toward redemption is necessarily one of suffering, with Christ as our model for how to revel and worship, suffer and sacrifice.

The denouement of *Four Quartets*, "the fire and the rose are one," runs parallel with events found in *The Divine Comedy*. Before Dante can enter Paradise, he must pass through a wall of fire.[4] The mere contemplation of this act is terrifying: "I lean forward over my clasped hands and stare / into the fire, thinking of human bodies / I once saw burned, and once more see them there."[5] Personal experience can impede our own redemption. Dante's

---

1. Eliot, *Four Quartets*, 59.
2. Ibid.
3. Ibid.
4. Dante, *Divine Comedy: Purgatorio*, Canto 27.
5. Ibid., 348.

past keeps him from heaven's future. It is only when Virgil (Dante's guide) reassures him that Dante is able to step into the furnace. "Within that flame / there may be torment," Virgil says, "but there is no death."[6]

Suffering is the only path to the empyrean. There is no shortcut apart from the *passion* Christ embodies and invites us to. Dante's vision of Immanuel, God with us, is found in the Mystic Rose, "a white rose, the host / of the sacred soldiery . . . / all those whom Christ in his own blood espoused."[7] John Ciardi's brilliant English translation adds a second layer to the Italian word *sposa* ("to marry/bride") with *espoused* here, a clear association with adoption, even as it retains the English *spouse*. Marriage and adoption become the two central images for the kingdom of God. As in Paul's letter to the Ephesians, *eros* and *agape* are glimpses of the life to come. In the Webster family, adoption has been a foretaste of heaven's economy, a portrait of God's love for us *while we were yet sinners*, the rebels of God.

My mother's letter ends with a kind of prayer. "I will not forget you," she writes. "I can only have faith now that the world will be kind to you and that you will find strength to withstand it if it is not." Her words reflect the struggle of trying to love in a fallen world. The mystery of adoption resides in her promise never to forget, even as she entrusted me to the only parents I've ever known. Her prayer fills me with unparalleled gratitude for the Webster family, and for the revelation of finding her letter in a file cabinet all those years ago. If a central thesis of *Four Quartets* is that "human kind / Cannot bear very much reality,"[8] then adoption is a manifestation of our capacity to love, despite the challenges we face. Two loves stayed Solomon's hand and raised me to adulthood, called me to a better life, called me their own. The fire and the rose are one.

---

6. Ibid., 349.
7. Ibid., 584.
8. Eliot, *Four Quartets*, 14.

16

Open Questions

Michael Dean Clark

I hear adoptive parents say this all the time: as soon as I saw her, I knew she was the one. I know it's self-centered, but I tend only to believe that about my story. Because that's exactly what happened. At least when I tell the story.

Our adoption started with a picture from an orphanage we knew little about in an African country we'd never visited. But there she was, six weeks old, resting on the shoulder of one of the women taking care of her until we could. A tiny baby, she had enormous eyes, the look in them calmer than it should have been. I was working at the time, so I called my wife and told her she needed to check the Web site I was looking at because I'd found the girl who made me want to be a father. Our Klarissa.

Her name means "gift," and that's exactly what she has always seemed to be to us. I can remember praying for her health, her safety, for the process to go smoothly, for our ability to be parents to a girl who would need the reassurance that we would always be there for her. Her biological mother died giving birth to her, and her birth father made the awful but necessary decision to give her up so that she could survive.

He never knew how quickly that would be necessary. We only found out years later. At two weeks old, just days after she was taken to the orphanage in Freetown, Sierra Leone, eighteen hours from the village where she was born, Klarissa contracted malaria. She was taken to the hospital and the people who worked at the center didn't know if she'd ever come back. She did. Three weeks after that, I saw her picture, and we started the process of adopting her.

At that point, it was supposed to be quick. Six months, maybe nine at the outside. But then it took more than two years. There were two trips to Sierra Leone, multiple occasions when it seemed we would never complete the adoption, and the heart-wrenching experience of having her for more than two weeks—just long enough for her to start calling us Mama and Dadda—only to be forced to take her back to the orphanage and fly back to America without knowing if we'd ever come back.

And then it was over. A judge granted our adoption order, the consulate in Senegal processed her visa, and a judge in California made it official here. Our little girl was ours, as much as any child is ever her parents'. In my head, we had been through the worst and what was left was the process of creating a sense of our new normal. But normal is always difficult, especially with adoption, and even though ours was about the smoothest adoptive transitions I've seen, I would learn later that the real work was yet to come.

Two things people need to know about Klarissa: she is precocious with words and with grace. When she came home at a little over two, she was using roughly fifty words in English, by our count. Within six months, she was over three hundred and talking more than most of the two-year-olds we knew. That hasn't stopped. She's a storyteller. It runs in her family.

So it seems more than natural to me that Klarissa, who has been in and out of college writing classes since she was four (a hazard of having a professor/father who likes to shame his students with his precocious child), started writing early. Her first stories were oral. When she was three, she told us the story of the Suspicious Cowboy, based on a character she was looking at on the children's menu of the steakhouse where we were eating. And yes, she could correctly define *suspicious*. We asked. A series of short books about a character named Mrs. Moonbeam followed, enough to give seven away as Christmas presents to family members. She illustrated them herself. And on it has gone, in journals and notepads and on napkins and in conversation. If I had to estimate, I'd conservatively put her total life page count at well over three hundred pages by the time she turned nine.

But all of those stories were fiction. And then she was asked to write about being adopted for a small magazine. This story was different. This was true. This was about her. This was going to be read by other people. The prospect scared her, but not as much as the topic. There were tears and fits and starts, but then she found something that needed to be said. That some of the stupidest questions, the most hurtful ones, always seem to be with her. With each new school and new friendship, she's never Klarissa. She's Klarissa the Adopted One. And this is where her propensity for grace comes in.

I have watched Klarissa act with grace in the way she deals with her brothers. If I'm honest, I've seen it in the way she deals with me as a parent. But watching her tackle a topic that is fraught with fear and uncertainty— all the questions she can't answer about herself and the ones she wishes people just wouldn't ask in the first place—that's been a clinic in grace. Grace in allowing us to see what she normally keeps to herself, and grace in confronting those questions within herself for an audience of readers who are likely to ask her those questions themselves.

When she was four, Klarissa began asking really tough questions about race and difference and family and home. I'm not sure I gave her satisfactory answers, so I wrote an essay imagining what it would be like to tell the sixteen-year-old future version of her the story the four-year-old one could not understand. Or maybe it was the one I was too afraid to tell her at the time. It started like this:

> *My daughter Klarissa loves to hear her story. She asks all the time. "What was it like when I was a baby? Did I used to do that too? Tell me again."*
>
> *I do every time, but I always feel guilty. Eventually, she'll realize I don't know her story. Not really anyway. At least, not the first two years of it. But I'm her daddy and I tell stories for a living. So I tell hers.*
>
> *It has become more difficult recently. Klarissa's a perceptive four-year-old given to remembering everything my wife and I tell her and using it against us. When our son was born, her questions changed.*
>
> *"Daddy, why does he look different than me? How come Holden can't be brown like me? What was it like when I was in Mommy's tummy?"*

I guess it's always been about questions for her. I often tell my students that being a writer is committing ourselves to the moment we are in; that it is challenging ourselves to keep life from sliding away from us unnoticed, for ourselves and our audience. As I put it in another place, "[Writing] is a transaction between the storyteller and the audience, and the currency is understanding." I tell Klarissa this too, praying that someday her own answers to the hard questions she's so often faced with, the ones she finds as she writes her life story, will be sufficient. And as I do, I find the end of my old essay even truer now than it was when I wrote it.

> So I think, if I had to end the story for her right now, I'd tell her this:
>
> "Honey, you need to learn to write soon so you can come up with the ending that makes you happy."
>
> I guess that'll work no matter how old she is when I actually tell her this story. Or maybe I'll just leave the last page blank and let her fill it in herself. I'm sure her version will be better than anything I come up with. And yet, as I write these words, I feel a fear that comes only as regularly as her questions. Eventually, she'll have control of her own story. Actually, if you listen to the details of her planned wedding to Prince Ali, you'd see that Klarissa already has her hands in creating the narrative of her life.
>
> And the fear grows with every fairly tale she tells. How many stories will she see in her own?
>
> We like to believe our stories happen to us, that we're merely recording the "truth." But we make our stories, bending them to our perception. And so will she.
>
> How many characters will she edit? Or add? Or delete? How many will she move to an appendix because they aren't important enough to be part of the primary story arc? In some stories, Mom is central. In others, she's an unmarked grave in the forests of West Africa. But what place will that grave hold in Klarissa's tale? And what place will her adopted Mama have? Or me for that matter?
>
> And there is the root of my fear. I guess it's common, one most parents experience as their children grow up. At what point do we become irrelevant? And yet, I can't help feeling that the nature of a family created by adoption is different; that the danger of our being written out in favor of all the things she'll never know about her imagined life is somehow more likely.
>
> And no, the irony of my job is not lost on me. I guess all I can really hope for is a line in her dedication.

Six years later, Klarissa's now a ten-year-old who writes for publication, and I still have the same fears. Fortunately, the older she gets, the more my daughter's gift for including everyone in the life story she's writing becomes apparent. So I get up each morning looking forward to seeing what unfolds in her next chapter.

17

Dumb Questions about Adoption[1]

Klarissa I. Clark (Age 10)

Kids ask a lot of questions. If you don't believe me, just talk to my younger brothers for five minutes. Most of their questions are about how things work, so they're not that bad. But sometimes, the questions other kids ask me are bad. As an adopted child who has parents of a different color, the questions I'm asked can go from annoying to hurtful or even tormenting. When I think about all these questions, the only word I can use to describe them is *dumb*.

Some people say there is no such thing as a dumb question, but I disagree. Dumb questions about being adopted are the worst because they put a lot of pressure on me and make me feel sad, different, hurt, and misunderstood. This is especially true at school. To be clear, when I say "dumb questions," I mean questions that I can't or shouldn't have to answer because they don't really feel like questions at all.

I'm just finishing fourth grade, and every day it feels like classmates pester me with these types of questions about adoption, like "Are you adopted?" If they bothered to look at my family, the answer is so obvious they wouldn't have to ask the question because my dad's skin is peach and mine is extra frothy mocha. An equally obvious question came when a boy in my class saw me with my dad and asked, "Is that your real dad or your

---

1. A version of this essay appeared in the fall 2012 edition of *Viewpoint*, the alumni magazine of Point Loma Nazarene University.

babysitter?" This made me feel like everyone was looking at me, like I was an oddball. Another question that really hurt was, "Did you know most terrorists are adopted?" Honestly, I felt like punching the kid who said that in the nose, but I didn't.

Even though a good comeback phrase can feel great to send right back at a dumb question, it's better to have a conversation about it with the person or with your parents. Here is an example of that type of conversation. If someone on the playground or at lunch asks, "Did you know that most terrorists are adopted?" you just calmly say, "I don't think that's true! I think you said that just to be mean and that is flat-out rude." Some questions turn into statements, like when you're arguing about something completely different they'll say something like, "Adopted children are stupid." Questions and statements like this make it hard to answer. Kids use them just to throw you off and give themselves time to win the argument when they think that they're losing. This is why these types of questions bother me. They aren't really being asked to get to know me.

Dumb adoption questions put a lot of pressure on me because they usually come before teasing. This bothers me because being teased about adoption is very hard for me. It makes me feel sad about losing my birth mom and how my birth father couldn't take care of me. When I'm done, I feel like I was left out in the rain, and I see my life as a total debacle of unfortunate events. But it's not. My life is full of love from my family and God. My mind is a field that has survived fires. I know that God helps us with our problems because God has helped me.

Instead of dumb questions, there are many important questions I wish people would ask me. For instance, they could ask if I have brothers and sisters in my family. Or they could ask if my adoptive parents are nice or mean. Do they let me wear makeup to school? Would my parents let me have a sleepover? These last two are important because they would be helpful in deciding if we could hang out more and what we would do together if we could.

I bet that you've noticed that I'm not answering the family questions. I haven't been answering them because then that whole paragraph would be all about me and seem sort of like I'm writing fan fiction about myself. That would take your focus off the types of questions that would be worth asking and won't hurt a person's feelings.

I like these questions because they're just friendly ways that someone might use to strike up a conversation, ones I'd be willing to answer here.

Maybe I'd even prefer questions about what I'm into, like what kinds of music do you like? (Anything except country and rap.) Have you been to any concerts? (Yes, but I'd like to go to more.) What movies are you allowed to watch? (A lot of Steven Spielberg but no HORROR!) Do you have a cute, surfing boyfriend? (No, but I hope I get one soon!) Or others like have I ever kissed someone? (Yes, my next-door neighbor when I was five.) They could even ask if I drink soda on Sunday or read in bed. These questions aren't stupid because they would help people see me, and if someone were to ask me one of these questions in public it wouldn't shatter my dignity. I'd prefer these questions because these questions seem normal, they're not mean, and they're not about Africa. If I talk about where I'm from, I want it to be my choice to do so.

Just before I turned ten, I was asked to write my story, this story, for a magazine. After the article was published, my teacher asked if I would share it with my class. When I did my classmates made me feel special and understood, but at first it didn't really seem to change much. It just made people want to be my partner in everything at school because the article showed that I'm smart. But I also learned that my classmates (even the boys) saw that adoption is serious and that it makes people vulnerable to bullying.

This made them more sensitive, so that's a good thing.

The bottom line is that people don't want to be known as different. For example, if someone is missing a leg or arm she doesn't want to be called The Kid without an Arm or Leg. It's the same with adoption. I don't want to be defined as The Adopted Girl. I want to be known as a person who is funny, cute, and interesting, not the girl in the mush pot with everyone in the circle looking down on me because I live in a different family than the one I was born into. What dumb questions have taught me is that we shouldn't look down on each other. We should treat each other equally.

18

Grit and Grace

BETH WOOLSEY

The snow fell hard and heavy in our little Oregon town, a novelty for those of us accustomed to perpetual drizzle. I finished the grocery shopping with three small kids in tow, a little bit self-congratulatory, a little bit twitchy, and a lot exhausted as I struggled to push the loaded cart through the slush and sludge. It was no small thing, literally or figuratively, to move my children and myself through an unfamiliar landscape in pursuit of sustenance. Most days, our family of five was stitched haphazardly together with a complicated mix of faith, doubt, and stubborn determination, and it's fair to say we were all a little unsure of our footing.

Seven months earlier, Greg and I had adopted our second and third children—our son, Ian, and our daughter Aden—from Guatemala. Compared to our first adoption, our daughter Abby at just a few weeks old from Vietnam, Ian's and Aden's adoptions at ages three and one were like an elementary school exercise in defining contrast. Where Abby's entry into our family was happy, Ian's and Aden's were heartbreaking. And where Abby's attachment took days, Ian's and Aden's took years. Their adjustments were, I hasten to add, neither to Abby's credit nor Ian's and Aden's fault. It was, simply, an entirely different experience bringing home a healthy infant than bringing home two toddlers with developmental delays and nutritional deficiencies and medical issues and night terrors and tremendous bewilderment.

The Spirit of Adoption

I often prayed as we navigated the first days and months of Ian's and Aden's adoptions. When the prayers had words, they usually sounded like this: "Oh my God, what have we done?" It was a strange prayer for one who had believed adopting our kids was God's will for us all. Billy Graham said that "the will of God will not take us where the grace of God cannot sustain us." But as the months passed, I felt like I was babysitting strangers rather than parenting my children, and I began to wonder whether it was God who took us to these kids or me with my fingers in my ears yelling *la la la* and ignoring God entirely. My theology at the time still allowed for a vindictive God who, if I didn't make each life choice precisely according to the Divine (but murky) Prescription, would watch me flounder on that path, shaking his head in disappointment and *tsk-tsk*ing with increasing volume until I could hear him over my apparent self-centeredness and unwitting disobedience.

I suppose I thought if these adoptions had, indeed, been God's will, I would feel more certain, the adjustment would be less agonizing, and all of us would feel strong. Instead, we were weak, every last one of us laid bare and flailing.

"Oh my God, what have we done?"

We call Ian our Prolific Puker, our Heroic Hurler, our Super Spewer, these days in admiration and as a badge of honor for all of the times he so brilliantly made it to a container—*swoosh! no rim!*—but early on in dismay. Ian vomited every time he was nervous. Or excited. Or upset. Or confused. And there's almost no situation for a developmentally delayed three-year-old who is abruptly removed from his culture and language that isn't heavy with excitement, anxiety, and confusion. It was a season flooded in vomit.

While Aden took to me immediately and refused to let me set her down awake or asleep for the first year, Ian did not. Ian was uncertain about me and wanted nothing more than for me to go far, far away and leave him with his dad, with whom he felt much more comfortable. Whenever I came in the room—you guessed it—he puked.

"Oh my God, what have we done?"

Surely God didn't mean for this to happen: for my son to live in fear of his mother and for me to be unable to reach my son. And I never felt more like a maternal failure than when I buckled Ian into his car seat. There was just no way to avoid close proximity in that situation, and nothing was more distressing than watching my son reel back, squeeze his eyes closed, and gag.

I couldn't shake the feeling that we'd wronged Ian by adopting him. That no child should have to be so scared. That another mother would have found a way to connect.

We muddled through that first half-year. Abby turned six and detested sharing us with the new parent-poachers. Ian turned four without the ability to communicate verbally. Aden was one and showed no signs of walking. My husband, Greg, and I missed each other on nearly every level. Isolated and weary, we hadn't found our way back to each other yet.

This was the family I unloaded from the grocery cart on that wet, snowy day. I told Ian and Abby to climb into the van while I regretted choosing plastic grocery bags, which were sure to fall over and spill everything on our way home.

And then there was blood. The snow was too slippery or the traditional push-past-the-sibling move got out of hand and the next thing I knew Ian's head hit the edge of the sliding door. Hard. The blood cascaded from his forehead and splashed on the snow. The gash wasn't huge, but it was deep. Ian was scared, and I wasn't sure he could let me console him.

I moved the way mamas in an emergency move. Quickly. Breathlessly. With my stomach upside down. I left my groceries in the cart. I left my purse. I left the van wide open, and I rushed back to the store with the baby on one hip, my son cradled awkwardly on the other with his head pressed to my breast in a futile attempt to control the bleeding, and I herded Abby ahead of us.

A wide-eyed teenage clerk rallied to help us find an unused checkstand with a phone where I sat on the floor and telephoned for help. And as I waited for my friend to come drive us to the hospital, a woman I didn't know with snow in her hair handed me my purse—and grace. "I put your groceries in your car," she said. "I locked your van, and your keys are in your purse." And then she said, "You're doing a good job, mama. You're doing exactly right."

I held Ian at the hospital later while the doctor stitched the gash closed. I immobilized my son with my arms, our faces inches apart, my blue eyes looking into his pools of brown, and he didn't gag even once.

In the past ten years, I've stopped it with the vindictive God theology and the either/or proposition of God's will or my own. I've come to believe life, including our choices and our faith, is more collaborative than that. And I would change Billy Graham's quote just a little; there is nowhere God's grace cannot sustain us, no matter whose will takes us there. God's grace doesn't look the way I thought it would. Not like easy. Or like it all works out in the end. No. God's grace looks like a woman with snow in her hair who is kind to a young mom. And like a friend who drops everything to rush to the hospital. And like a raggedy child with his head pressed to his mama's chest, brown eyes seeking blue ones, both blurred by tears. Grace looks like steps that are sometimes agonizing and slow, pushing through the slush and the sludge, trying to find the way even in the midst of pain.

"Oh my God, what did we do?"

I know the answer now.

We built a family.

We built a family the way all families are built. With desolation and consolation. With doubt and faith. With weakness and strength. With grit and grace.

19

A Tapestry of Redemption

One Adoptee's Journey

KELLI HALL

One of my favorite birthday traditions is to listen to my parents tell the story of my arrival. While at work, my mom got a phone call announcing that her baby girl was born. She called my dad at work, relaying the news and telling him to come pick her up right away. Dad turned white as a sheet and left the office in a rush. He and my mom went out to lunch prior to making their way to the adoption agency, discussing baby names and contemplating how their lives would be forever changed that day. When they arrived at the agency, my mom heard a baby crying and silently hoped that this cry was not coming from her child. The staff told my parents that I had given them quite a time of it, to my mom's dismay! But as the adoption worker placed me in my mom's arms, I immediately stopped crying. I believe that God must have prepared me to know that these people were my parents, people in whom I could trust.

My parents say they did not know the first thing about caring for an infant. They had no diapers or clothes, no ready-and-waiting nursery. They were told not to prepare too much ahead of time, since there was no way to know for sure when or if they would receive a child. One of their first stops with me was to visit a friend, who asked if my parents had burped me. When my parents said no, not knowing how to do this, their friend showed them how to burp me and change my diaper. My parents brought me to my grandma, who joyfully watched me while they went shopping for baby necessities.

My parents told me of my adoption before I could understand its meaning, and always in a positive manner. One of the statements I heard most often was that I was twice loved: loved by my birth mother, who decided to place me for adoption to give me the best life possible, and loved by my parents, who wanted to raise a child. My parents provided me with the information they were given: my birth mother was young and not married, and my birth parents wanted me to be placed in a Christian family where I would be the oldest child. During the rigorous adoption application process that explored every facet of their lives, beliefs, and plans for child rearing, my parents disclosed with some hesitancy the importance of their Christian faith. They worried that their honesty about this might have adverse consequences. However, it turned out that their decision to share their faith led the adoption caseworker to match me with my parents.

A comment that my mom made has stuck with me over the years: I ultimately belong to God and not to my parents. God gave me to my parents to care for me for however long God allowed, and the more people who loved and supported me throughout my life, the better. Over the years, my parents, especially my mom, asked if I had questions about my adoption or thought about my birth mother. I remember feeling somewhat awkward when this topic was brought up. I usually had nothing to say, as I did not think about it very often—being adopted was a normal, accepted fact of life for me. At the same time, I felt comfort in knowing that my parents were open to talking about it at any time. As I grew older, I heard and read stories about individuals who did not find out about their adoption until they were teenagers, or found a picture or document tucked away somewhere that uncovered this secret. I am extremely grateful that I always knew the truth and could incorporate that truth into my life as I grew.

In elementary school, when students were asked to share something unique about themselves, I often shared that I was adopted. Usually, this disclosure would solicit the popular question, "Have you ever met your birth parents?" When I answered no, this was typically followed by, "Do you ever want to meet them?" Although I was not necessarily annoyed by these questions, I found them quite predictable. It seemed that others were timid when asking, as though the topic were taboo. But I had no reason to feel uncomfortable. I had nothing to hide—no shame or guilt—surrounding my adoption.

Though I do not really look like my parents, my adoption is not obvious, either. The same is true of my younger sister, adopted from a different birth family. On more than one occasion when on outings with my sister, a store clerk or shopper has observed our interactions and commented that we must be sisters. We look at each other with a knowing smile and respond, "Yes, we are!" I enjoyed teasing others with a riddle about my ethnic heritage: my dad is Finnish and my mom is German and Swiss—what does that make me? Biologically, I am German, and I think there was something comforting about sharing part of my mom's heritage. My parents, neither of whom tan well, shared openly the benefit of how my different genes allowed me to tan easily. Growing up in the Christian faith, I developed the belief that all Christians are adopted into God's family; adoption is a part of God's beautiful, redemptive plan. The messages I received from my parents, their support and openness, and my faith helped form in me a positive sense of self and identity.

I happened to grow up in a neighborhood where the families living on either side of us also adopted children. Two siblings had open adoptions and ongoing contact with their birth mothers. I remember thinking how confusing that would be, having two mothers with very different roles. From early on, my parents often assured me that they would help me search for my birth family if I made that decision—but I felt no inclination to do so. Though mine was a closed adoption, I had a letter from my birth mom (in addition to a brief medical history and non-identifying information about my birth family), which my parents made available for me to read at any time. Even throughout my childhood, I felt I would not be ready to read it until I was "settled" as an adult.

Once I was married and living away from my parents, I asked my parents to bring the letter when they visited for Easter that year. I read the letter privately in the bedroom, slowly taking in every detail. This letter confirmed my parents' mantra that my birth mother did love me and wanted the best for me. I felt incredibly blessed; the love my birth parents had for me was evident. The letter included a Scripture verse, and my birth parents wrote that they were open to hearing from me. My husband joined me later and, when I was ready, I sat between my parents on the couch as we talked about the letter. I was glad that I read the letter but still unsure of when or if to contact my birth parents.

I worked in a homeless shelter as a case manager after graduating from college and was struck by the thought that my birth mom may be homeless, or famous, or anywhere in between. I clearly remember the response of my colleague when I shared that I was adopted: "You turned out so well!" It sounded strange and made me wonder, why would I not turn out well? Shortly thereafter, I attended graduate school to pursue a degree in social work, where my developing professional interest in foster care and adoption intersected with an increasing personal desire to reach out to my birth mom. My primary motivation would be to assure her that I was well, that I had a wonderful childhood and family, and to thank her for the decision she made to give me life and make an adoption plan. But shortly after graduating, my husband and I moved, and I started a new job as a case manager for foster children and decided to pursue my social work license. Life was full and busy enough that I did not want to add a birth parent search to the mix.

The following summer, after obtaining my social work license, my mom came for a visit. I summoned the courage to express my curiosity about searching for my birth mother; though my mom provided the supportive response I expected, an enormous sense of loyalty to my parents made me wary of taking any steps that would inadvertently hurt them. It felt as though I was crossing into uncharted territory in our relationship. My mom readily gave me contact information for the woman who had been my adoption caseworker at the agency that had facilitated my adoption. My parents kept in touch with her through the years, especially early on. I accepted the information but did not act on it for several months.

That fall, I began talking to my husband in earnest about initiating the search process. One evening, after one of our conversations and after I had already gone to bed, my husband found a search inquiry on a website that revealed an entry about me! Knowing that I had a busy workday ahead, he anxiously withheld telling me about his discovery until the next evening. It was then that he asked to talk. With great seriousness he asked, "What if I know something about your adoption that you don't?" He told me about finding the search inquiry. Two names were listed; perhaps they were my birth mom's maiden name and married name, or perhaps the names of my birth mom and birth father. He asked if I wanted to know the names that he had seen on the website. I had mixed feelings initially, knowing that once I heard the names, the information would somehow change me forever. It seemed strange that my husband would know this information but I would not. I agreed for him to tell me. As I allowed these names to sink in, I broke out in tears—hearing the names of my birth parents made them all the more real. My husband showed me the website, and I stared at it, shocked and amazed that someone was searching for *me*.

Three weeks later, as my husband and I sat down to dinner, our phone rang. The person on the other end explained that she was a contract worker with the agency that coordinated my adoption. She said that her news might come as a surprise: my birth mom was searching for me and wanted to know if I was open to having contact with her. Though it was a shock to receive her phone call—it felt like an invasion of my privacy on our unpublished, seldom used phone line—it was no great surprise that my birth mom initiated a search, since I had seen the website inquiry just a few weeks prior. I told her that, although I had thought about contacting my birth mom, I was not ready to give a definite answer. Plus, I wanted to verify the contract worker's legitimacy before moving ahead.

The timing of these events amazed me. My heart was ready to begin the search process; otherwise, I would have responded with even greater hesitancy than I did. I wanted to talk with my parents about it, but our next few cross-country phone calls did not provide appropriate moments to discuss the topic. Finally, several long weeks later, I told them about the website inquiry and phone call from the contract worker. I felt awkward sharing this information, yet relieved at the same time, perhaps because it was not a typical conversation with my parents. They offered to contact my former adoption caseworker to get her perspective, to which I agreed.

The next night, my dad sent me an email detailing my adoption caseworker's response to the website inquiry and contract worker's call. She felt that the contract worker's phone call was very aggressive and questioned this method of contacting me. In her experience with searches, the adoptee is likely to be curious and just wants to know a bit more, while the birth parent is seeking a relationship; she warned that a desire to assure my birth mom that I am doing well might not be enough, and there could be significant pressure placed on me to become more engaged in an ongoing relationship. She added that this was not just a potential issue for me, but could significantly affect my whole family.

I called her soon after to discuss this further. Her advice was to be certain about what I wanted, to take it slowly, and to sit on any decisions before acting on them. If I chose to initiate contact, my adoption caseworker recommended that I do so through a trusted intermediary. I contacted the agency that facilitated my adoption and verified the contract worker's role. I wondered about my birth mom's motivation for contacting me at this time.

Was she ill? Did she need help? A worker at the agency shared that they had heard from my birth mom over the years, that she was anxious to know about me, and that she had finally decided to search. I learned that my adoption agency could forward letters to my birth mom without revealing my identifying information. After receiving this input, I decided to write a letter to my birth mom using an intermediary. It felt like the safest option. I read several books presenting various adoptee experiences and issues to consider regarding reunions. I prayed for wisdom and guidance, and for God to watch over my family and birth family in this process.

I finally sat down and wrote a letter to my birth mom in the spring, after allowing the holidays, filled with family gatherings and potentially emotionally charged, to pass. It was a Saturday, and I spent several hours working on it. I wondered how to even begin writing to the individual who arguably played the most important role in my life, yet who was a perfect stranger. I included in the letter that I wanted to take things slowly, as it takes me time to adjust to change, but that I was open to exchanging letters through the agency. I informed my parents that I had finally written it, and held onto the finished letter for a week.

I struggled through that week with the weighty decision of mailing the letter. Whereas I previously envisioned writing a letter to my birth mom that would remain in my adoption file unopened until the end of time, I now knew that it would actually reach her. Mailing it would mean giving up my control. Once the door of contact had been opened, I could never reverse it. I could not determine what came next, and my birth mom's receipt of my letter would change things forever. Would she accept me and like me? The question loomed over me. However, I knew in my heart that I needed to send the letter, regardless of the potential consequences. If my birth mom had any lingering doubts or pain from having relinquished me, I wanted to offer healing. When I dropped the letter off at the post office, I felt relieved that I did not have to agonize over the decision anymore. I then waited anxiously, wanting to hear something, wanting to be certain that she had received my letter. It was two weeks before I received a reply. When I read it, I felt an overwhelming sense of peace. I could not have anticipated the beauty of the reciprocal healing that awaited me in her words.

Through my birth mom's letters, I learned that she came to trust in God during her pregnancy with me, that she held me for two days in the hospital, whispering words of love and blessing over me. She prayed for me every day throughout my childhood and now reached out with the hope that we could share our lives as I felt comfortable. Her interests sounded much like those of my parents: remodeling, gardening, and entertaining. We, too, shared similar interests, and happened to live, unknowingly, in the same geographical area for much of my life. Living across the country at the time of this initial contact gave me a comfortable, natural boundary from which to learn about my birth mom. I was anxious to know what my birth mom's family thought of our contact—or even how much they knew about me at all. I was assured by my birth mom's words that she was proud to read about the person I grew up to be, that those close to her always knew about me and supported our contact, and that God answered her prayers more than she could have imagined. It was a relief to me, knowing that my birth mom was stable, doing well, and shared my faith.

Within eight months, my birth mom and I had exchanged a few sets of letters and decided to correspond through email. My birth mom asked me to send a picture if I felt comfortable. I asked if she would send one of herself first. Would I look like her? I grew curious to know if she had any pictures of herself while pregnant with me, or of us together when I was first born. Many of my friends by that time had birthed children. They all seemed to have joyful photos depicting the mom in the hospital bed holding the newborn and the dad leaning in; it struck me that I did not have any such picture of myself. We did exchange pictures, and though there was some resemblance between us, our biological relationship was not obvious. Though finally settling into the whole idea of having contact with my birth mom, I still felt a range of emotions about it. I carefully weighed what I shared about my family, wanting to be careful to respect their privacy. It was of critical importance to me to protect my parents in the process and give them the time they needed to adjust to this change.

Over the next year, my husband and I felt ready to grow our own family with children. I asked my mom if it would be sad for her if I had biological children, wondering if such an event would dredge up memories of my parents' infertility. Her response was an emphatic no. She always felt that God designed me to have a certain personality and physical characteristics that she and my dad could not give me, but also intended that my parents be the ones to raise me. She has always maintained that, if given the choice again, she would choose to adopt me. In fact, when mom learned about childbirth, she asked my grandma if there were any other way to have children. My grandma replied that people could adopt children. My mom never had a longing to experience pregnancy, as I did.

The Spirit of Adoption

During a summer visit to see family, with my husband's support and encouragement, I arranged to meet my birth mom in person two years after our first letter exchange. I was pregnant at the time; it seemed important to meet her before I had a baby of my own. I asked my parents and husband to join me, the four of us together, while my brave birth mom came alone. In our correspondence before meeting, my birth mom and I talked through our possible feelings and reactions to seeing each other; we would probably cry and want to exchange hugs. We met at a coffee shop and talked for two hours. Seeing her was surreal. She was gracious and sweet, just as she came across in her letters. Meeting her helped to take away the fears and doubts of the unknown, both for me and for my parents. My birth mom shared that around five months into her pregnancy with me, she felt very strongly that she was carrying me for a family. I believe this aided in my ability to experience such a congruent sense of self; I felt and heard the same narration from my birth mom and my parents.

My husband and I moved back across the country to be near both sets of our families shortly before our first baby was born. This was a big, wonderful change, since I had grown accustomed to seeing them only twice a year for the previous six years. It also brought my birth mom and me geographically closer, which intensified my strong sense of loyalty toward my parents. The opportunity to see my birth mom several times within the span of a year suddenly felt like too much, too soon. Despite our healthiness as individuals, navigating the relationships between and with my birth mom and adoptive parents proved very complex and delicate. I carefully communicated these feelings to my birth mom, not wanting to hurt her feelings. She responded with an understanding and grace that amazed me.

The next spring, after seeking my permission, my birth mom informed me that she had contacted my birth father and had his contact information for me when I wanted it. She relayed that he was glad to know I have had a blessed life and humbled to tears at the possibility of hearing from me. She communicated to my birth father that it is up to me if, when, and how much contact to have with him, and I felt grateful for this support from her. There may come a time when it is right to meet him, but that time has not yet arrived. That summer, my husband, son, and I, along with my birth mom, had the opportunity to meet my younger half-sister and her husband, who were visiting from out of state. My half-sister learned of my existence from my birth mom when she was twelve years old and always hoped for the chance to get to know me. Our meeting over lunch together at a restaurant was pleasant, like meeting the good friend of a friend. My knowledge of the happenings in her life comes through my birth mom, at least for now.

Around the same time, my birth mom started presenting options to meet her parents, whom she knew would treasure meeting me and my family. Their ability to travel was declining quickly, in addition to my birth grandfather's health. I soon realized that I did not want to miss the opportunity for us to meet each other in this lifetime. A few birth family gatherings were possibilities, including my birth grandfather's ninetieth birthday party, but my birth mom's large family (she being the seventh of nine children) intimidated me. Also, I did not want to become a focal point at these family events. Finally, over a year later, my husband, son, and I traveled to meet my birth grandparents in their home. My birth mom and her husband met us there. My birth grandmother teared up, sharing that the most difficult part about my adoption was not knowing what would happen to me. I discovered that I inherited my dimpled chin from my birth grandfather. A tour of their small home included a book shelf filled with family pictures, revealing a picture of my husband and me, and a picture of our son; this instilled in me a great feeling of being included and loved. My birth mom later shared that both she and her mom felt that meeting me completed a piece of them that was missing.

My adoption journey has not been free of challenges. After all, adoption is a response to something that is broken. At times, I feel frustrated that I and other adoptees have to confront issues that non-adopted people do not ever consider. Adoption is something that happened to me; though very grateful for it, I did not ask to add this complexity to my life. Yet, I find myself taking on the responsibility to make sure that the others involved in my adoption are faring well. I rather enjoyed the pleasant, predictable, and steady nature of the relationships in my family prior to my search and reunion. But I alone had the ability to extend words of healing to my birth mom and birth family, and I chose to accept that mantle.

Today I work as a mental health therapist, primarily seeing clients working through adoption- and trauma-related issues. Though grief, loss, shame, guilt, and trauma are common experiences of adoptees, I was spared from the injurious brunt of these by having parents who addressed these needs before I knew they existed. When therapeutically appropriate, I am honored when I can utilize my story—whether directly or indirectly—in ways that bring insight and education to adoptive parents, hope and healing to birth parents, and understanding and perspective to fellow adoptees. It is my hope that sharing my story honors my parents and birth mom, offers encouragement to individuals connected to adoption, documents this journey for my children and generations to follow, and acknowledges the hand of God in my life. For this is not just my story; it is one piece of the much larger picture of God's redemptive purpose for each of us.

20

Reflections on Adoption and Religion

RUSS RICHTER

Cleave is an interesting word. It means "to split apart," especially along a natural line or grain; and it means "to stick two things together," as we often hear in wedding ceremonies. The former definition of *cleave* seems to describe how a biological child enters her family—by being physically separated from her mother's body; the latter definition seems to describe how an adoptive child enters her family—by being added to (or fastened to) her parents. The resultant bond created by this *cleaving of children* is indistinguishable between the two "cleaving" methods.

Why We Adopt

In my experience, the motivation for adopting is usually some combination of three basic drivers: parental instinct, righteous intents, and providence.

Parental Instinct

When I was little, thanks to Jacques Cousteau's alluring accent and the exotic underwater images shown on his TV show, *The Undersea World of Jacques Cousteau*, I wanted to be an oceanographer. Later, an artistic talent surfaced, and my plans changed. I decided I wanted to be an artist, living a meager life in a French garret and pouring my soul onto canvases for the awe and wonder of the world. The realities of life displaced that desire, and my creative passions were redirected from oils and canvas to computers and code. The reader should note at this point in this brief discussion of "what do you want to be when you grow up" that, when asked to identify myself, I would do so in terms of my profession. Parenthood was not a part of the paradigm I had envisioned for myself.

Becoming a father has reversed that paradigm. My roles as a father to my two daughters and as husband to my wife eclipse my role as an employee. I see myself first as a husband and as a father. As a father, I have a responsibility to my children to prepare them spiritually and emotionally for this beautiful, hideous world so that they can safely experience the joys and sorrows it offers. I want them to be somewhat like me, but better—more courageous, more excited, more capable. They are burgeoning bundles of potential that deserve a directed, yet free expression, and it's my joy to help them manifest that potential in the most positive, rewarding way.

Oh, and I have a job, too.

Men and women both have that innate desire to parent. In my case, that instinct surfaced when I became a father, not before. Others desire to parent long before becoming one. Parenthood may satisfy our innate instinct to nurture. It may satisfy our desire to transform a young, tender life into a confident, responsible, productive member of society. Regardless, the desire to be a parent is an ingredient in the decision to adopt.

Righteous Intents

Given the choice, most of us want to do noble things for society. If we took average people off the street and offered them the opportunity to do something good for the world, or something destructive, most would choose to do something to make the world better.

So, when we consider creating or expanding a family, it's not surprising that we consider the adoption of orphans as a means toward making the world better. Orphans, we understand, are nothing like Annie of movie, stage, and comic book fame. By and large, we believe that orphans, whether they are generally ignored in an orphanage crib or live with a foster family, have been cheated out of a forever family. Their lives are inherently unstable. Perhaps they are bonding with a temporary "family" from which, they know, they will someday be taken. Perhaps they are not bonding at all, but are living as children disconnected from the loving bonds of family.

There are probably points along the continuum between these extremes. But, none of those points can be considered anything but an injustice to the child. Children deserve a single, stable family that will nurture them, protect them, teach them, encourage them, inspire them—in short, love them. As we decide to bring a child into our lives, we consider the noble, righteous option to adopt as one of the ingredients in that decision.

Further, we must include in this section of righteous intent a religious aspect that may drive some toward adoption. In Judaism, for example, adoption is considered by many to be one of the greatest mitzvot (commandments, or good deeds done from religious duty). The Talmud, which is the compilation of rabbinic opinions explaining the Hebrew Bible, expresses the mitzvah of adoption clearly in *Sanhedrin* 19b in which rabbis explain that when someone raises a child in his home, it is as if he had begotten that child. In other words, from a scriptural perspective, those who raise another's child are the child's parents just as if they had borne that child.

To illustrate this, rabbis cite several scriptures. Naomi's widowed daughter-in-law, Ruth, bears a child, Obed, who is raised by Naomi. Naomi's neighbors declare, "Naomi has a son!" Though Ruth bore the son, Naomi raised him, and thus he was called Naomi's son (Ruth 4:17). In another example, we see that Michal, daughter of King Saul, never bore any children (2 Sam 6:23). But, we also see a mention of the five sons of Michal (2 Sam 21:8), whom she raised for Adriel, the husband of her sister, Merab (who may have died). So, Merab bore the children, and Michal brought them up, so they are ascribed as Michal's sons.

Several other cases are included in the Talmud to support and illustrate that those who bring up a child in their home are the child's parents. The point is clear: from a Judeo-Christian perspective, raising an adopted child is a noble, righteous duty blessed by God—a mitzvah.

Interestingly, a "mitzvah" is sometimes interpreted, at least colloquially, as a "blessing," and it's not hard to find the dotted line that would connect "a commandment from God" to "a blessing." Jewish families understand the mitzvah of adoption. When we are out with our two obviously adopted daughters, Jewish women are apt to comment about our adoption saying, "It's a mitzvah," intending, I think, both definitions. They recognize the meritorious act as well as the blessing our children are to us.

The Spirit of Adoption

Providence

Some may call it *fate*. Some are fascinated by the Chinese Red Thread theory, summarized in a proverb: "An invisible red thread connects those who are destined to meet, regardless of time, place, or circumstances. The thread may stretch or tangle, but will never break." (My wife has embedded that proverb in her email signature.)

Some may subscribe to *chaos theory*. Recall the famous example of a butterfly flapping its wings in China, causing a ripple effect that eventually creates a tornado in the United States. With the proper understanding of nature and events, we would be able to trace the effects to the causes all the way back to the butterfly's wings.

Some may ascribe it to a *divine plan*—a trajectory of events preordained by the Almighty. "God works in mysterious ways," as the saying goes. God does things his way and in his time, and He tends to do them in ways that seem to be intentionally confusing to us. The Bible is rife with examples. Joseph was sold into slavery by his brothers, and ended up in jail. But, we see later that God had planted him in Egypt in order to rescue Israel from the famine in Canaan. Moses was abandoned by his mother and adopted by an Egyptian princess, became a fugitive from Egypt, and returned to rescue Israel from Egypt. Jesus was killed in a horrendous, agonizing way. But it was done to rescue us all from sin.

If we accept these grand examples of prophecy and fulfillment, then we should also accept the prophecy/fulfillment concept on a smaller, more intimate scale. That is, if God can plan for an exodus of his people four hundred years in advance, or the salvation of humankind five thousand-plus years in advance, then it's reasonable that God could also plan for a couple to adopt a particular child.

My daughters understand that, even though they grew in another mommy's tummy, that they were made specifically and exclusively for our family. We have equated their abandonment with a letter being placed in a mailbox. In other words, they were not discarded by their birth mothers. Instead, they were set on a journey to us, their forever family.

In a nutshell: "Not abandoned. Delivered."

Our family believes in the inscrutable nature of God's providence. The more we pay attention to the causes and effects in our life and the more we pay attention to our history, the more we see God's hand at work in our lives. From this hindsight, we gain understanding; from understanding, we have faith; from faith, we have peace. This peace quells the temptation to second-guess our decision to adopt. We know that God endorsed and/or directed the adoption of our daughters. So, we don't have to worry about whether or not we did the right thing.

But, this can be approached from a more practical perspective, too. In his daily *News and Comments* radio show, when telling stories of beheading, maiming, burning, amputating, and other atrocities that were perfectly acceptable forms of punishment in other cultures, but were horrifying to US sensibilities, Paul Harvey often would say simply, "It is not one world." It was his way of reminding us that people in the United States had a different view of life, God, society, and culture.

Our daughters were both born in China. China's one-child policy and preference for sons are responsible for so many daughters being abandoned. While we strolled the streets of China with our first daughter in our arms, several Chinese women stopped us to take a peek at her. They would invariably ask with their limited English, "Girl?" and then comment, "Lucky baby." We would respond that we were the lucky ones to have been blessed with her, but they would point at her and repeat more emphatically, "Lucky baby!"

When we got back to Texas and went to Chinese restaurants, the waitresses would often ask us about our new baby, and would echo the comment we heard in China: "Lucky baby." And, we would respond with our usual "No, we're the lucky ones." One waitress finally explained it to us. "She is a lucky baby because she is alive."

In China, when a daughter marries a son, she goes to live with her husband and his family. She works her in-laws' land and cares for them as they grow old. This tradition, when coupled with the one-child policy, creates a social condition in which sons are prized and daughters are useless. Having a daughter means you have no son to work your fields, and no one to take care of you in your old age. Giving birth to a daughter is a curse. For this reason, it is said that there is often a bucket of water nearby when a Chinese woman goes into labor. If the baby is the "wrong" sex, a surreptitious visit to the water bucket is an expedient way to remove that curse and to give her another chance at a having son. It bears repeating that it is not one world.

The girls who survive in China are truly lucky. Some of these girls are accepted by the family, especially rich families in big cities. Other survivors are placed in cardboard boxes and left in public places where they will be found and taken to social welfare institutes, otherwise known as orphanages. This is done at great peril to the mothers (or the agents) because it is illegal to abandon children in China. These mothers know their daughters are too costly to keep, but also know they are too precious to destroy. So, they send their daughters on a one-way journey, not knowing where they will end up, but hoping they will be delivered to a better situation. ("Not abandoned. Delivered.")

Our Chinese guide for our second adoption noticed something about our younger daughter. She had been marked with a sharp tool in a semi-visible location. We didn't notice the marks until she pointed them out to us. She explained, "They are so her Chinese mother may know who she is, if someday they run into one another." This is the unselfish love and hope of a mother who wants only the best for her baby.

No, it is not one world. But, neither is China one nation. Some in China would dispassionately dispatch an infant for the seeming crime of being female, while others would go to extreme measures to deliver their daughters from that horror. In this, we maintain the hope that someday, China's one-child policy will be abolished. In the meantime, we accept as a blessing that our daughters have been delivered to us, more likely by God than by red threads or butterfly wings.

This belief in providence, I propose, is the third ingredient in a decision to adopt. If you believe it is God's plan for you to adopt, then you are likely to decide to adopt.

In any decision to adopt, there are varying quantities of these three ingredients—parental instinct, righteous intents, and providence. We have a desire to be parents (otherwise, why adopt?), and adoption in itself can be a noble act, fulfill what has been predestined, or both.

Effects of Adoption on Religion and Faith

After we married, my wife and I tried unsuccessfully to conceive. After several infertility treatments, we finally got pregnant with twins, but miscarried. This was a devastating end to our hopes of having a baby. So, we decided to adopt, and a series of events brought us to international adoption, and ultimately to China. This process did not go easily, either. At the time, the adoption process in China from log-in date (when China officially receives your family dossier and starts the process of matching you to your child) to your referral date (when China contacts your agency to inform you of a matched child) took about six months. Thanks to the Internet and social media, we were able to track our progress through the process along with other families with similar log-in dates. Our anticipation grew each month as the list of referral dates came out. Finally, we saw that our referral date was sure to be in the next batch. Excitement filled every minute of every day as we prepared the baby's room and did all those silly things that giddy, expectant parents do.

Then, the unexpected happened. When other families with similar log-in dates started getting their referral phone calls, we got a call from our agency informing us that they accidentally didn't send our dossier to China six months prior, that it was still on their desk in Kansas, and that we would need to redo some of the paperwork that had expired before they would send our dossier to China. So, when other families who had waited six months for their referrals were flying to China to adopt their children, we were sent to the back of the line to start over, this time wallowing in tears, anger, and frustration.

At every turn, our attempts to become parents seemed to be more difficult and more heart-wrenching than for those around us. Our friends and family were procreating with ease, and we were suffering the indignity of infertility treatments and the horrors of miscarriage. Adoptive parents were winging their way to China and bringing home their precious babies, and we were sent back to the beginning to start paper-chasing, again.

Were we doing something God didn't want us to do? Should we abandon our attempts to have a baby? To adopt? Why would God do this to us? More than once, we looked at our faith and had to decide which definition of "cleave" to apply to it. Would we hold more firmly, or separate from it? We were like Job, rebuking God for treating us unfairly.

Once we finally got to China, and the China Center of Adoption Affairs director called for Family #3 (us) and the orphanage nanny put our daughter in our arms, we understood that things happen for a reason, and at the right time. God, as any good parent will do, taught us to be patient, to have faith, and to be humble. This little girl—this exact little girl—was chosen just for us. No other child in our adoption group would have suited us as well, and it's likely that no other child in any prior adoption group would have suited us well as this one child, who crossed her fingers and ground her teeth, and smiled that first morning when she woke up for the first time in her life with the same people she had fallen asleep with the night before.

Of course, we decided immediately that this daughter should have a sibling, and as soon as we were able, we submitted our dossier again.

Our second adoption had more setbacks. The non-special needs (NSN) program in China was winding down, and the usual six-month wait had grown. After a year, we started to lose that exciting feeling of anticipation. After two years, we became frustrated. After three years, we had lost hope. We were angry, frustrated, sad, and a bit desperate. Again, we took God to task for not listening to our prayers and for ignoring our pleas. "You said, 'Knock and the door will be opened. Ask, and you shall receive.' But, it doesn't seem like you're following through on that promise!"

Truly, we had not yet learned our lessons in patience, faith, and humility. Being no closer to a NSN referral, it made no sense to continue to wait, and we decided to investigate the special needs children, which ultimately brought us to our second beautiful daughter. With her wry smile, flashing eyes, and exuberance, she was also clearly made for us. Once again, in hindsight, we saw that God was working in a time not of our own. God's plan for us needed to play out, and it was also important for us to learn—relearn—our lessons in humility and faith.

I'm embarrassed to admit that we are not done learning these lessons yet. (But, we're not dead yet, either. So, there is still hope for us.) We continue to be set upon by apparent misfortunes (job loss, diagnoses, etc.), and we again turn toward heaven and channel Job. We point our fingers at God, and in rage and fury demand, "Why do you treat us like this? Why are you doing this to us?" And, when the passion subsides and we are exhausted from rebuking the all-knowing, all-powerful, all-loving God, we look at our daughters and humbly, sheepishly say, "Oh yeah. That's why." There is no better example of God's endless love for me than in teaching me—personally, me, myself—about humility and faith.

A Cousin at the Dinner Table

Before becoming a father, I read the passages in the Christian Bible that refer to being adopted as children of God, and I viewed them, naturally, from the perspective of the adoptee.

> Yet to all who did receive him, to those who believed in his name, he gave the right to become children of God. (John 1:12)

> For those who are led by the Spirit of God are the children of God. The Spirit you received does not make you slaves, so that you live in fear again; rather, the Spirit you received brought about your adoption to sonship. And by him we cry, "*Abba*, Father." The

> Spirit himself testifies with our spirit that we are God's children. (Rom 8:14–16)

> But when the set time had fully come, God sent his Son, born of a woman, born under the law, to redeem those under the law, that we might receive adoption to sonship. Because you are his sons, God sent the Spirit of his Son into our hearts, the Spirit who calls out, "*Abba*, Father." (Gal 4:4–6)

When I read those passages, I understood I had been accepted into a really big family with many brothers and sisters, and that I am one of God's children. God is the adoptive parent, and I am the adoptee. I spent very little time thinking about that relationship. I had a natural father and understood my relationship with him from the child's perspective, and this seemed essentially the same kind of relationship. I rely on him for my essentials—love, shelter, food, education, and so forth. My dad provided for me, taught me to hunt and build and plant and find my way when I was lost, and played with me ("42" being a family favorite).

But, was an adopted child as valued and loved as much as a biological child? If I had thought about it at the time, I would probably have said, "No." Parents simply must cherish their biological children more than their adopted children. They may teach the same things to their biological and adopted children, may play the same games with them, and may provide for them the same way. But, the love for the child who is "flesh of my flesh" surely must take precedence over the love for the child that "came to live with us."

Confession time: I come from a traditional family—one dad, one mom, four sons, none of whom was adopted. In fact, growing up in rural Texas, I didn't know anyone who was adopted. Adoption, to my limited frame of reference, was taking in an orphan and caring for him or her. But, because the orphan was born of different parents, the adoptive parents certainly would value the adoptee somewhat less than their biological offspring. I was clueless and ignorant.

So, even though I read that I was adopted as a child of God, I still considered myself somewhat less valuable than a "true" child of God. I was lucky to be part of his family, to be provided for, and to enjoy the benefits of the family, but made no presumptions about my station in that family. I was "different" than his family. I was accepted into his family, but was still different, and therefore, separate—like a welcome cousin at the family dinner table.

However, after adopting our first daughter, I experienced a dramatic shift in perspective. I suddenly saw my "adoption relationship" with God from the point of view of the adoptive father—from God's point of view! This was a breathtaking epiphany. Dorothy's Kansas was black and white and shades of gray. But, when she entered Oz, her world instantly became drenched in vivid colors. My realization was like that. My pallid perception of my "adoptive father/adopted son" relationship with God suddenly took on a depth I had not previously recognized or anticipated. Those things I had seen before in monochrome became richer, and the gray things I had not been able to differentiate before were suddenly clearly defined. It was the difference between listening to a song on a scratchy record played on a Victrola phonograph, and standing live in front of the Houston Symphony Orchestra, engulfed in a resonating crescendo of thunderous basses, violins shouting to heaven, timpani rolling like thunder, brass screaming with joy, and cymbals exploding like fireworks. I finally got it.

My daughters look different than me. I am Caucasian; they are Asian. But they are not, by any stretch of the imagination, "cousins at the dinner table." They are my daughters, whom I love with the colors of Oz. They are my family, and my love for them is complete and unfettered. Adoption is irrelevant.

With this new perspective, I no longer see myself as a cousin at God's dinner table. If God has adopted me as a child, then I am a full son of God's. Because I understand my love for my daughters, I now better understand the depths of God's complete and unfettered love for me.

The Sin of Being an Unwed Mother

I remember seeing a bumper sticker that read, "How much sin can I get away with, and still go to Heaven?" At the time, it made me laugh, and then wonder: How much sin *can* I get away with? There must be some threshold of sin that will prevent me from passing through the pearly gates. I was young. So, I hadn't discovered that's not how the Christian concept of sin and heaven work. (Thank goodness!) But, I once heard a parable that helped me better understand it. A man was presented with two wine glasses. In one was poured a fine, red wine, to which was added a few drops of sewage. In the other glass was poured a generous portion of sewage, to which was added a few drops of fine, red wine. Of course, the man rejected both glasses as they were now both sewage, and therefore, undrinkable.

Metaphorically, we are all glasses of wine and sewage. We are not worth drinking. That is, we are all sinners and are not worthy of Heaven. "How much sin can we get away with and still go to Heaven?" becomes a rhetorical, even deceptive question. In fact, "The wages of sin is death," according to the apostle Paul. Not, "the wages of 'big' sins is death, and 'little' sins are okay." Rather, all sin leads to death, implying all sins are equal—from murder to lying, from fornication to lust, from worshipping other gods to stealing. Sin, all sin, results in death. It is not some threshold of sin we must stay below that makes us worthy of Heaven because all sin makes us unworthy. Instead, it is the amount of forgiveness that makes us worthy of heaven.

A baby conceived as a result of a sinful act is an interesting phenomenon. If all sin leads to death, this particular sin is unique in that it also leads to a new life! This dichotomy probably deserves more thought and its own thesis, but it is included here so readers may consider this in their contemplations about unwed mothers and their children.

I have never been in a church that condemned unwed mothers. I assume those churches exist somewhere. But, I have been fortunate enough never to have found myself in their pews. The churches I have attended have had genuine concern, rather than condemnation, for unwed mothers. An unwed mother has enough to deal with and doesn't need to be fussed at by holier-than-thou rabble. She needs compassion, love, and guidance.

To those Christians and churches that would condemn a woman for being pregnant out of wedlock, I would offer this pearl of wisdom, which also came from a bumper sticker: "Jesus condemned not sinners, but hypocrites."

Conclusion: Do the Best You Can

When my oldest daughter tries to do something difficult, something she's likely to fail at, I tell her, "Do the best you can with what you've got." After all, you can't do any better than "the best you can," and you can't use more than "what you've got." What more can we expect?

I think that's the philosophy we use with adoption.

In China, the mother has an agonizing process to go through. She gets one chance to have a child, and for her family's sake, it must be a boy. But, she has no control over the sex of her baby. She carries a baby nine months, and when she at last realizes she has given birth to a daughter, she must do the best she can with what she's got. Depending on her circumstances, "the best" could mean secretly delivering the girl to an orphanage.

A couple dealing with infertility issues decides to adopt. This decision means an orphan gets a family, and a family gets a child. But, with international adoption comes many challenges: bonding; grieving; remorse; ambiguous family health history; culture confusion; racism. Yet, it's the best they can do with what they've got.

There clearly seems to be some injustice in this common scenario. A mother in China bears the scars of a necessary decision. A Chinese-born daughter in the United States dwells on her own scars inflicted by a mother who would abandon her (incidentally, giving little thought to the complicit Chinese father), and then contemplates the motives of the parents who would adopt her. Adoptive parents try everything they can to negotiate the convoluted, dynamic network of feelings their daughter is experiencing at any given point in her development, just trying to make it all better. Social and economic pressures in China created this cauldron of angst. So, it is difficult to point the finger of blame for this situation at any one person (other than Mao Zedong, perhaps).

Of course, China is not the only country with orphans. Socio-economic conditions in many countries result in babies languishing in orphanages. HIV/AIDS and wars in African nations compound the socio-economic problems leaving children without parents. The United States, of course, has its share of orphans, though traditional orphanages have mostly been replaced by parents willing to foster (as my wife's family did for many years). While those social, political, medical, and economic issues are being addressed by the countries of the world (a plodding process, to be sure), we must not forget the innocents—the orphans, who, through no fault of their own, go to sleep each night with no mother and no father to love them.

In the end, we all do the best we can with what we have. In life, events transpire in unpredictable, uncontrollable ways. Whether they are caused by God, good intentions, poor judgment, or butterfly wings, sometimes things just happen. How we choose to deal with those things will define who we are as individuals, as families, as a society, a culture, a religion, a nation.

Bibliography

Alighieri, Dante. *The Divine Comedy*. Translated by John Ciardi. New York: Norton, 1954.
All God's Children International. "The Global Orphan Crisis." 2013. https://www.allgodschildren.org/orphan-care/the-global-orphan-crisis.
Buechner, Frederick. *Wishful Thinking: A Seeker's ABC*. New York: HarperOne, 1993.
Burke, Trevor J. *Adopted into God's Family: Exploring a Pauline Metaphor*. Downers Grove, IL: InterVarsity, 2006.
Canlis, Julie. *Calvin's Ladder: A Spiritual Theology of Ascent and Ascension*. Grand Rapids: Eerdmans, 2010.
Charity Water. "Why Water?" 2013. http://www.charitywater.org/whywater/.
Cruver, Dan, ed. *Reclaiming Adoption: Missional Living through the Rediscovery of Abba Father*. CreateSpace, 2010.
Eliot, T. S. *Four Quartets*. New York: Harcourt, Brace, 1971.
Farmer, Paul. *Pathologies of Power: Health, Human Rights, and the New War on the Poor*. Berkeley: University of California Press, 2005.
Fessler, Ann. *The Girls Who Went Away: The Hidden History of Women Who Surrendered Children for Adoption in the Decades before Roe vs. Wade*. New York: Penguin, 2006.
Groody Daniel G. *Globalization, Spirituality, and Justice: Navigating the Path to Peace*. Maryknoll, NY: Orbis, 2009.
Habitat for Humanity. "About Habitat for Humanity." 2013. http://www.habitat.org/how/about_us.aspx.
Hamlin Fistula International. "What Is a Fistula?" 2012. http://www.hamlinfistula.org/what-is-a-fistula.html.
Holy Qur'an. Translated by A. Yousuf Ali. Hertfordshire, UK: Wordsworth, 2001.
International Justice Mission. "Who We Are." 2013. http://ijm.org/node/46.
Medical Teams International. "What We Do." 2013. http://www.medicalteams.org/what_we_do.aspx.
Munsch, Robert, and Sheila McGraw. *Love You Forever*. Scarborough, ON: Firefly, 1986.
Murray, Anne F. *From Outrage to Courage: Women Taking Action for Health and Justice*. Monroe, ME: Common Courage, 2008.
Pinnock, Clark. *Flame of Love: A Theology of the Holy Spirit*. Downers Grove, IL: InterVarsity, 1966.
World Vision. "Our History." 2013. http://www.worldvision.org/content.nsf/about/history.
———. "Our Impact: Education." 2013. http://www.worldvision.org/our-impact/education.

www.ingramcontent.com/pod-product-compliance
Lightning Source LLC
Chambersburg PA
CBHW030859170426
43193CB00009BA/675